Restoration
COMEDY
1660 – 1720

Restoration
COMEDY
1660–1720

BY

BONAMY DOBRÉE

OXFORD UNIVERSITY PRESS

Oxford University Press, Ely House, London W.1.

GLASGOW NEW YORK TORONTO MELBOURNE WELLINGTON

BOMBAY CALCUTTA MADRAS KARACHI DAR ES SALAAM LAHORE DACCA

CAPE TOWN SALISBURY NAIROBI IBADAN

KUALA LUMPUR SINGAPORE HONG KONG TOKYO

FIRST EDITION 1924
Reprinted lithographically in Great Britain by
LOWE AND BRYDONE (PRINTERS) LTD., LONDON
from sheets of the first edition

1938, 1946, 1951,
1955, 1958, 1962, 1966, 1970

To

ALAN LUBBOCK

CONTENTS

I

INTRODUCTORY

Drama and Values.

IN the history of dramatic literature there are some periods that can be labelled as definitely ' tragic ', others as no less preponderatingly ' comic ', though of course both forms exist side by side throughout the ages. Taking the period of Aeschylus, Shakespeare, and Corneille as markedly ' tragic ', we find that these writers throve in a period of great national expansion and power, during which values were fixed and positive. At such times there is a general acceptation of what is good and what is evil. Out of this, as a kind of trial of strength, there arises tragedy, the positive drama; there is, as Nietzsche suggested, ' an intellectual predilection for what is hard, awful, evil, problematical in existence owing to . . . fulness of life '.

In the great ' comic ' periods, however, those of Menander, of the Restoration writers, and at the end of Louis XIV's reign and during the Regency, we find that values are changing with alarming speed. The times are those of rapid social readjustment and general instability, when policy is insecure, religion doubted and being revised, and morality in a state of chaos.

Yet the greatest names in comedy, Aristophanes, Jonson, Molière, do not belong here: these men flourished in intermediate periods, in which the finest comedy seems to be written. In form it still preserves some of the broad

B

sweep of tragedy, and is sometimes hardly to be distinguished from the latter in its philosophy, its implications, and its emotional appeal. Think of *The Silent Woman* or *Le Festin de Pierre*. In this period we find that tragedy has lost its positive character, and begins to doubt if the old values are, after all, the best. It begins to have a sceptical or a plaintive note, as in Euripides, Ford, and Racine. Values are beginning to change ; they are not yet tottering.

Keeping this in mind, let us cast a cursory glance at the nature of comedy.

Comedy.

Everybody will agree that *Othello* is not a comedy, and that *The School for Scandal* is not a tragedy. But on the other hand *Volpone* is at least as different from Sheridan's play as the latter is from Shakespeare's. Similarly, in the period under consideration, Etherege's *The Man of Mode* is not at all the same kind of thing as Wycherley's *Plain Dealer*, though both are called comedies. Again, if we are certain of the mood we get from *Lear* or *The Importance of Being Earnest*, what are we to say of *Measure for Measure*, *Le Tartufe*, or *Le Cid*?

It is not surprising, then, that no theory of comedy yet developed, from Aristotle to Meredith or M. Bergson, seems to cover all the ground ; and for the purposes of this book it will be useful to distinguish three kinds of comedy, or at least three elements in comedy. This is not to elaborate a theory, but to provide a standpoint from which we may obtain a clearer view of the works we are about to consider.

1. *Critical Comedy*. The vast bulk of comedy is of the ' critical ' variety. What, for instance, was Aristophanes

Critical Comedy

doing but ' to laugh back into their senses " revolting " sons
and wives, to defend the orthodox faith against philosophers
and men of science ' ? Menander, to judge from Terence,
was doing the same kind of thing, as was Terence himself.
This is the classical comedy from which much modern
comedy is derived. It sets out definitely to correct manners
by laughter ; it strives to ' cure excess '.

This comedy, then, tends to repress eccentricity, exaggeration, any deviation from the normal : it wields the
Meredithian ' sword of common sense '. It expresses the
general feeling of the community, for which another name
is morality ; it is, to quote Meredith again, the ' guardian
of our civil fort ', and it is significant that when comedy
has been attacked, it had always been defended not on
aesthetic but on moral grounds. But the defence has never
been very successful, for the morality preached by comedy
is not that of fierce ardour, of the passionate search after
the utmost good, that in itself is excess, and subject for
comedy (e. g. *Le Misanthrope*); but, as we continually find
from Terence to the present day, it supports the happy
mean, the comfortable life, the ideal of the *honnête homme*.
Its lesson is to be righteous, but not to be righteous overmuch, which in the mouths of those who hold the doctrine
becomes

> J'aime mieux un vice commode
> Qu'une fatigante vertu.

Its object is to damp enthusiasm, to prick illusions. It is
in a sense prig-drama ; it flatters the vanity of the spectator, for whose amusement the weaknesses of his friends
are held up.

One might imagine that confronted with comedy clothed
in the garb of conscious virtue, the writers of comedy themselves would cry ' Fudge '. But these, in the seventeenth

century at least, always fell back upon the moral argument,
as though they lacked the defiance of their raillery. Jonson
declared that comedy was ' a thing throughout pleasant
and ridiculous, and accommodated to the correction of
manners ', saying in the preface to *Epicene* :

> The ends of all, who for the scene do write,
> Are, or should be, to profit and delight!

a charming alternative, of which, fortunately, he sometimes took advantage.   Molière, in his preface to *Le
Tartufe*, implicitly accepted the position when he wrote,
' If the use of comedy is to correct the vices of men . . .',
as though merely restating an unquestionable axiom. ' One
can easily put up with a rebuke,' he said, ' but one cannot
bear chaff.   One may have no objection to being wicked,
but one hates to be ridiculous.' Corneille, however, declared that ' Dramatic poesy has for object only the delight
of the spectators ', but he was forced to add that Horace
was right, and that everybody would not be pleased if some
useful precept were not at the same time slipped in, ' et
que les gens graves et sérieux, les vieillards, et les amateurs
de la vertu, s'y ennuieront s'ils n'y trouvent rien à profiter '.

In the period we are about to survey, the same ground
was taken up. Shadwell, in attempting to continue the
tradition of the Comedy of Humours, wrote of Jonson :

> He to correct, and to inform, did write.
> If poets aim at nought but to delight,
> Fiddlers have to the bays an equal right,

a statement which reveals Shadwell's limitations as clearly
as his point of view. Congreve and Vanbrugh—Wycherley's
moral purpose is overwhelmingly evident in three of his
plays—stimulated by Collier's declaration that ' The business of plays is to recommend virtue and discountenance

vice', were loud in their protestations. Congreve even
forestalled the frenzied divine in his preface to *The Double
Dealer*, where he said ' it is the business of the comic poet
to paint the vices and follies of humankind '. Vanbrugh in
his heart thought that the object of plays was to divert, and
to get full houses, but he accepted the moral standpoint in
his *Short Vindication*, saying, ' the business of comedy is to
show people what they should do, by representing them on
the stage doing what they should not '. Who would refuse
to be moralist on those terms? Farquhar, modifying the
claims of comedy, declared in his preface to *The Twin
Rivals*, ' that the business of comedy is chiefly to ridicule
folly ; and that the punishment of vice falls rather into the
province of tragedy ', thus curiously forestalling Coleridge,
who thought wickedness no subject for comedy.

Indeed the description of the morality as ' a play en-
forcing a moral truth or lesson ' might almost be taken as a
definition of any comedy that deals with types, or ' humours'.
For comedy, in so far as it is a generalization, can scarcely
avoid type, and once this form has been, accepted, the
pontifical robes of the moralist descend almost inevitably
upon it.

The foregoing may throw a light upon why it is that
comedy appears when it does. Comedy of this type is not
a phosphorescent gleam upon the surface of a decaying
society, but a conservative reaction against change. It is,
in short, a social corrective.

2. *' Free ' Comedy*. There are, however, some comedies
which seem to produce quite a different effect in us,
comedies in which we feel no superiority, and which incul-
cate no moral, but in which we seem to gain a release,
not only from what Lamb called the burden of our perpetual
moral questioning, but from all things that appear to limit

our powers. Of this kind of comedy, the plays of Etherege and Regnard are perhaps the best examples, though much of the laughter of Aristophanes is evoked in the same way. Here we feel that no values count, that there are no rules of conduct, hardly laws of nature. Certainly no appeal, however indirect, is made to our critical or moral faculties. We can disport ourselves freely in a realm where nothing is accountable ; all we need to exact is that the touch shall be light enough. We take the same delight in the vagaries of Sir Fopling Flutter as we do at the sight of an absurdly gambolling calf. Judgement, except the aesthetic, is out of place here. We are permitted to play with life, which becomes a charming harlequinade without being farce. It is all spontaneous and free, rapid and exhilarating ; the least emotion, an appeal to common sense, and the joyous illusion is gone.

I have named this comedy 'free' because it depends upon there being no valuations whatever ; it is possible only in a world where nothing matters, either because one has everything, or because one has nothing. Since it can afford to be careless, it can be completely unmoral. Etherege wrote in the first exuberance of the return from exile of a court to which no moral argument could appeal. In the *Chanson Faite à Grillon* Regnard wrote :

> Il sera gravé sur la porte :
> Ici l'on fait ce que l'on veut,

a motto that might be prefixed to each of his comedies. And if the above are examples of free comedy written by those who had everything, the Commedia dell' Arte may stand as an example of that performed by those who had nothing, and which flourished most when the spectators and actors had least ; for when there is nothing more to be lost, there can be no further responsibility. Life and its appropriate comedy can be perfectly free.

3. *Great Comedy.* There is, however, a third comedy, perilously near tragedy, in which the balance is so fine that it seems sometimes as though it would topple over into the other form, as in *Volpone* or *Le Misanthrope*. And here to leave the instances definitely recognized as comedy, are not *Troilus and Cressida* (Shakespeare's), *Measure for Measure*, and *All's Well that Ends Well* also of this kind? Is not Mr. Shaw right in regarding *Coriolanus* as the greatest of Shakespeare's comedies? Indeed the really great figures of comic literature can hardly be thought of apart from their tragedy : who can regard the melancholy knight of La Mancha without pity, or disentangle the elements of the tales that beguiled the road to Canterbury?

The greatest comedy seems inevitably to deal with the disillusion of mankind, the bitterness of a Troilus or an Alceste, the failure of men to realize their most passionate desires. And does not this enable us to come to some conclusion as to what comedy really is? Cannot we see from the very periods in which it arises in its greatest forms with what aspect of humanity it needs must deal? It comes when the positive attitude has failed, when doubt is creeping in to undermine values, and men are turning for comfort to the very ruggedness of life, and laughing in the face of it all. 'Je suis le rire en personne,' says Maurice Sand's Polichinelle, 'le rire triomphant, le rire du mal.' There he represents 'great' comedy.

For comedy does not give us anything in exchange for our loss. Tragedy moves us in such a way that life becomes rich and glowing, in spite of pain and all imaginable horror, perhaps because of them. In tragedy we are left in admiration of the grandiose spectacle of humanity stronger than

its chains, and we are reconciled when a Cleopatra, hugging
the asp, whispers: Peace, peace!
    Dost thou not see my baby at my breast
    That sucks the nurse asleep?

In tragedy we are made free by being taken outside the life
of the senses into that of imaginative reality.

Comedy makes daily life livable in spite of folly and
disillusion, but its vision, though as universal, is not that
of tragedy, for it laughs at the spirit as much as at the flesh,
and will not take sides. Tragedy is all that is commonly
said of it, in depth, revelation, and grandeur; but comedy
is not its opposite. The latter is not necessarily more
distant from life, nor is it life apprehended through the
mind rather than through the emotions. Neither is it the
triumph of the angel in man over our body of the beast, as
one has said, nor, to quote another, the triumph of the beast
in man over the divine. It is nothing so fleeting as a triumph.
It is ' a recordation in man's soul' of his dual nature.

Goethe sought in art courage to face the battle of life.
But it is doubtful if life is a battle, or a game, or a chaos
through which we walk with slippery feet. And comedy
gives us courage to face life without any standpoint; we
need not regard it as a magnificent struggle nor as a puppet
play; we need not view it critically nor feel heroically.
We need only to feel humanly, for comedy shows us life,
not at such a distance that we cannot but regard it coldly,
but only so far as we may bring to it a ready sympathy
freed from terror or too overwhelming a measure of pity.

These prefatory remarks may serve as a pivot from which
to survey Restoration Comedy.*

---

* As further examples of ' great' comedy I would give *The
Widow's Tears* of Chapman, and Calderon's *La Vida es Sueño*. In
modern times there are *Peer Gynt*, *The Playboy of the Western
World*, Tchekov's plays, and *The Dynasts*.

II

THE FRAMEWORK

LET us first examine briefly the soil in which this comedy grew.

The most hasty student of history regards the quarter-century succeeding the Restoration as one of unbridled licence, in which everybody from the king downwards was corruptible. He learns that morality was in abeyance, or at least submerged under a flood of not altogether joyous wickedness, and that 'polite' society was engaged in consciously living to the top of its bent, determined to extract what pleasure it could out of life. But this, of course, was not true of the whole community; it never could be, because always, somewhere beneath the surface, the normal life continues, quiet and self-possessed. Even about the court such men as Evelyn could exist, such women as Dorothy Osborne and the one who became Margaret Godolphin. But the lurid picture is at least superficially true of the society with which we have to do, that is, the society which patronized the theatre; amid the galaxy of wit and fashion all was at sixes and sevens, in politics, religion, and social convention.

We need not concern ourselves with the political and religious outlooks, for these are reflected in the state of society, and it is the last which interests us as students of the comedy of the period. Here we find that the elegance of court life, 'which for its politeness and pomp astonished Grammont, accustomed though he was to the magnificence of the French court', scarcely covered the complete absence of any standard of sexual morality. Charles, indeed, set the fashion, Pepys reporting of Mrs. Stewart that the king ' gets into corners, and will be with her half an hour together, kissing her to the observation of all the world '. Courtiers took the hint in a manner familiar to the most superficial student of memoirs of the period, so that ' the names of Buckingham and Rochester, of Etherege, Killigrew, and Sedley ', as Bishop Wilberforce once wrote, ' still maintain a bad pre-eminence in the annals of English vice '. Yet the interesting thing is that these men were not only wild gallants, but have a certain place in English literature. Buckingham wrote, or at least assisted in writing, *The Rehearsal*, and adapted Fletcher's *The Chances* ; Rochester, a strong and subtle mind, made poems that certainly outshine those of ' The mob of gentlemen who wrote with ease ' ; Killigrew was the author of several comedies, while Sedley adapted Terence, wrote an original play, and some charming poems, one of which begins with the immortal couplet :

> Love still has something of the sea
> From whence his mother rose.

These reviled rakes, then, were men of taste and of cultivated refinement. Buckhurst, afterward Lord Dorset, was a great patron of poets, and wrote the famous ballad ' To all you ladies now at land '. And in those days it did not seem absurd that Buckingham and Rochester should each, on dying, gain the solemn praises of Bishop Burnet.

It is idle to insist upon the licence of the times. If we read Hamilton's *Memoirs of Grammont*, an ' exquisite picture of manners ', as Gibbon called it, we can get a clear notion of the general attitude. Court ladies went about masked ; duchesses disguised themselves as flower sellers to visit their lovers in the early morning. Miss Jennings (sister of

the famous Duchess of Marlborough) and Miss Price arrayed
themselves as orange women to visit Rochester, who was
masquerading as an astrologer so as to catch some city
lady. Miss Hobart and Miss Temple exchanged dresses
and paraded masked in The Mall to befool the same extraordinary peer; and these were all court ladies. Bishop
Burnet tells of the court masquerades, and how even the
king and queen attended masked balls incogniti, 'and
danced there with wild frolic'. Nor was this the most.
Although poisoning never attained the vogue it did in
France at this period, Sir John Denham's wife was supposed
to have been poisoned 'by the hand of the Countess of
Rochester with chocolate'. Whether this was true or not,
the fact that it could be recorded by Aubrey is sufficient
indication of the morality of the time, while Burnet was
strongly inclined to believe that Charles II died by the
same foul means. When the actor Mountford was mur-
dered, little pains were taken to bring the murderer to trial,
and his noble accomplice, Lord Mohun, was acquitted.

To us it seems a fantastic world, brutal and stupid, for
all its merriment and grace; did not Rochester, Buckhurst,
and others break up the astronomical balls in Whitehall
for fun? Its pleasures seem to smack somewhat of effort,
and these men and women to express only a part of mankind in contrast to the wholeness of the Elizabethans.
That is the obvious aspect. Yet can it have been just
that? What really underlay this behaviour that seems to
us so extraordinary? For at bottom, men do not deliberately
live this troubled life, existing from day to day. Certainly
people were determined to enjoy their newly regained
luxury and security, and besides, nobody could foretell what
the morrow would bring: at any moment the king, in spite
of a contrary determination, might once more have to go

upon his travels, for ' everybody, nowadays ', Pepys wrote, ' reflect upon Oliver and commend him, what brave things he did, and made all the neighbours fear him '. It was, maybe, preferable to have a Cromwell at Whitehall than to see the Dutch at Sheerness. But there was something deeper than this; and what we find, if we analyse the social behaviour of the time, is a great curiosity and a desire to experiment.

For it was an age of inquiry and curiosity: in it criticism became active for the first time. It had, indeed, existed before, but it had never had much effect. Now, however, writers were beginning to inquire how plays should be constructed, and what was meant by good English; they became conscious of what they were doing, too conscious perhaps. Not only do we find men like Dryden at one end of the period and Dennis at the other busying themselves with such questions, but also a host of virtuoso aristocrats. And just as literary curiosity was general, so was the scientific, and it was at this time the Royal Society was founded. If political experiment was at an end (it had assumed fantastic shapes), political curiosity was not, as witness the wide diffusion of the writings of Hobbes, Harrington, and Algernon Sidney.

This curiosity extended itself to everyday life; men and women were experimenting in social things; they were trying to rationalize human relationships. They found that, for them at least, affection and sexual desire were quite separate, and they tried to organize society on that basis. Love, in which the two feelings are imaginatively fused, scarcely existed for them. And since they accepted man as a licentious animal, it meant, of course, that if life was to be easy, the pursuit of a mistress must be an acknowledged amusement. You could, they believed, preserve your affection for your wife and be sure of hers for you, even if she had liaisons with other men. It was absurd to make a fuss about a thing that mattered so little. What then became of jealousy? It was ridiculous. Chesterfield, for instance, made jealous by the Duke of York's attentions to his wife, which had, indeed, been set in motion by her brother, sent her to the country and took as his confidant Hamilton, himself Lady Chesterfield's lover. The unfortunate husband obtained little sympathy. 'All over England a man who was so ill-bred as to be jealous of his wife was regarded with amazement; in the town, indeed, it was an unheard-of thing for a man to resort to those violent means to prevent that which jealousy both fears and deserves. However, people made what excuses they dared for poor Chesterfield, without laying themselves open to public opprobrium, laying the blame on his bad education. Every mother prayed God fervently that her children should never set foot in Italy if it meant they would bring back the ugly habit of restricting the liberty of their wives.' Thus it comes that throughout Restoration comedy husbands are such 'filthy, odious beasts' that it is hardly polite to mention them.

There is exaggeration here, one will say. Yes, and it was just this exaggeration that lent itself to the comic writers. Moreover, it was because the experiment did not, after all, make for social comfort that those who attempted it became the butts of the comic stage. For most men still disliked being cuckolded, the wittol was still an object of scorn. As a result of the conditions the jealous man became still more jealous, and fell into 'excess'. Had the experiment succeeded, there might have been no good Restoration comedy. Luckily such does exist, good serious comedy, concerning itself with something very important, in fact, eternal, for this question is never settled. Thus its bawdry is not merely jesting—though some of it undoubtedly is—but an attempt to be frank and honest. In this society of an experimental temper, seeking to see itself clearly, anything might be, and was said.

Restoration comedy, then, expressed, not licentiousness, but a deep curiosity, and a desire to try new ways of living. But since this question of ' impurity ' has been so much a matter of controversy, it may be treated separately.

Its Impurity.

' I could never connect these sports of a witty fancy ', Lamb wrote in his famous essay upon this comedy, ' in any shape with any result to be drawn from them to imitation in real life. They are a world of themselves—almost as much as fairyland. . . . They break through no laws of conscientious restraints. They know of none. They have got out of Christendom into the land of—what shall I call it ?—of cuckoldry—the Utopia of gallantry, where pleasure is duty, and the manners perfect freedom. It is altogether a speculative scene of things, which has no reference whatever to the world that is.'

But that this is untrue, even his admiring contemporaries had to admit. ' Perhaps ', Leigh Hunt commented, ' he thought that he could even play his readers a child's trick, and persuade them that Congreve's fine ladies and gentlemen were doing nothing but "making as if". Most assuredly he was mistaken.' Lamb's trick, indeed, was innocent enough ; he was trying to persuade his readers to become Congreve's also, in spite of their prudish horror. For Leigh Hunt was right ; and Macaulay, though his moral judgement was irrelevant, was not wrong in his facts : ' A hundred little tricks are employed to make the fictitious world appear like the actual world.' And Hazlitt in a brilliant passage showed that although this comedy might have no reference whatever to the world that is, it was very like a society that had been; 'we are almost transported to another world, and escape from this dull age. . . .'

Lamb's delightful argument does of course contain a useful truth; we must not confuse moral and aesthetic values. But it would not be of great importance at the present day in connexion with Restoration comedy were it not that many critics accept his dicta blindly; it is constantly assumed that to appreciate Restoration comedy we must accept Elia's attitude. Yet if we read this comedy in Lamb's spirit, we shall certainly find it very refreshing, but we shall miss seeing what it really was.

It is admittedly tiresome, but it seems unavoidable, to have to approach this work through Collier and Swift, Johnson, Macaulay, and Taine, and excuse its 'impurity'. For 'impurity' was its most important subject. How could it avoid dealing with sex when the distinguishing characteristic of Restoration comedy down to Congreve is that it is concerned with the attempt to rationalize sexual relationships? It is this that makes it different from any other comedy that has ever been written; but if we regard it as creating a wholly fantastic world we shall not see this. It said in effect, ' Here is life lived upon certain assumptions; see what it becomes.' It also dealt, as no other comedy has ever done, with a subject that arose directly out of this, namely, sex-antagonism, a consequence of the experimental freedom allowed to women, which gave matter for some of its most brilliant scenes.

'Sex in Congreve', Mr. Palmer says, ' is a battle of the wits. It is not a battlefield of the emotions '; but this was so in real life as well as in the plays of Congreve. 'When sex laws remain rigid . . .', writes Mr. Heape,* 'while society becomes more and more complicated and the life led by its members more purely artificial, the probability of the growth of drastic sex-antagonism is vastly increased, becomes indeed, a certainty.' But although men recognized with Hobbes that in the political world liberty and security are incompatible, and that a compromise has to be made, they did not see the necessity of applying the maxim in the social world. Men may not want the bonds of marriage, but once married they want to keep their wives to themselves. Women may be inconstant, but they want to be secure. Thus 'virtue' retains its social prestige. This was perfectly understood in those days, and was exquisitely phrased by Ariana speaking to Courtal (Etherege, *She Would if She Could*, v. i): 'I know you would think it as great a scandal to be thought to have an inclination for marriage, as we should be believed willing to take our freedom without it.' Indeed, a woman's virtue was of great importance, unless she was one of the king's mistresses. Says Lady Fidget to Horner (Wycherley, *The Country Wife*, iv. iii): 'But first, my dear sir, you must promise to have a care of my dear honour', because (v. iv) 'Our reputation! Lord, why should you not think that we women make use of our reputation, as you men of yours, only to deceive the world with less suspicion?'

But if sex did indeed become a battle of the wits rather than a question of the emotions, it must not be assumed that the figures represented on the stage were any less flesh and blood than their human types. Certainly, and here is the importance for us, the audiences did not regard the actors

* *Sex Antagonism*, by W. Heape, F.R.S.

as puppets playing at a life of their own, but as men living an existence which they were almost invited to share.*

But let us repeat that the object of the bawdry in these plays was not to tickle the desires of the audience. The motto of Restoration comedy was not ' Thrive, lechery, thrive ', nor its subject the successful pursuit of the town coquette by the town gallant, though this provided many scenes. Its great joke was not ' and swearing she would not consent, consented '. It had a profounder philosophy. Its joke, indeed, is rather a grim one ; it is more accurate to say that it is

> How nature doth compel us to lament
> Our most persisted deeds,

for having consented, she regretted ; he, having instituted liberty, repented of it.

But apart from these considerations, and apart from Lamb, does not the whole question of impurity, and any attempt to justify it, seem a little absurd ? For even if we abhor the idea of sexual looseness in real life, this does not preclude the possibility of turning the common facts of life into art. No one objects to ' adultery being part of the action ' in *Agamemnon*, *The Rape of Lucrece*, or *Anna Karenina*. And just as in these works something definite is made of the theme, so in our period the writers of comedy who were also artists, crystallized sex excitement into a comic appearance. Therefore the only questions arising are these : If we are disgusted at the ' impurities ' which are the material of much of this comedy, are they handled with sufficient skill to make us indifferent to the subject-matter ? Or is there, in spite of much that disgusts us, enough beauty and intelligence to overbalance our revulsion in

---

* As is made quite clear by the Epilogue to *Marriage à la Mode*.

C

favour of delight? Or can we simply accept the life of the time, and without associating it with ourselves, derive interest and pleasure from the observation and understanding of men whose outlook on life died with their erring bodies some two centuries ago? Surely this seems the reasonable attitude. Indeed, condemnation at this distance, emotion at two hundred years, itself provides a target for the comic imps.

Its Realism.

The question of realism, however, is one that claims our interest from other points of view; the obvious one, for instance, of structure, of how the men of that period set about writing comedy.

But a more important point is that of purpose. If comedy wishes to be immediately critical, two courses are open to it; either it can be fantastic, as with Aristophanes, or it must be realistic. Hence, in the latter case, the title of the Comedy of Manners. If it wishes to be critical in the larger sphere, it need not be realistic, and then it becomes the Comedy of Humours. And once more, where Restoration comedy is concerned, Lamb has queered the pitch. No one until his day doubted its realism; but nowadays it seems hard for a critic boldly to affirm it, for fear of being charged with not having read Elia. Its immediately critical intent made truth to external nature a necessity.

Evidently the way to clear up the question is to refer to the facts themselves, to see if the manners as we know them corresponded with what was put upon the stage. And indeed, a superficial reading of these plays, combined with a very small acquaintance with the period, will convince us that this comedy came as close to real life as possible, not only in its setting, as Macaulay insisted, but in the actual personalities and events. Naturally, the more inventive the artist the less can his models be found in real life, but the figures of Wycherley and Congreve are not so far removed from those of Shadwell and Vanbrugh that they seem to belong to a different world. This is not to say, of course, that comedy did not exaggerate; but its artificiality is only the artifice necessary to that concentration of life upon the stage wherein the art of the drama partly consists.

At once, with Etherege, we find portraiture, and from the first the characters in *The Man of Mode* were matter for controversy. Who, it was asked, was Medley supposed to represent? Was it Sir Charles Sedley? Was it perhaps Rochester? St. Evremond on his part declared Dorimant to be Rochester, while Dean Lockier said that 'Sir George Etherege was . . . exactly his own Sir Fopling Flutter, and yet he designed Dorimant, the genteel rake of wit, for his own picture'. Sir Fopling, however, was probably Beau Hewitt, 'the most notorious fop of the day'. Thus at that time it was not considered impossible to connect that sport of a witty fancy with a personage in real life. The example set by Etherege was followed by his successors. It is not, of course, fair to take such deliberate satires as Bayes in Buckingham's *Rehearsal*, or Antonio in the comical scenes of *Venice Preserved*, which were shafts too obviously directed at Dryden and Shaftesbury, respectively. Yet when Vanbrugh created Lord Foppington, he did not merely adapt Sir Fopling Flutter and ennoble Sir Novelty Fashion, but largely took as his model the famous Beau Fielding and copied him faithfully, even to the duel scene in which the hero received so harmless a scratch. Shadwell's Sir Positive At-All was supposed to be a caricature of one of the Howards.

Or again, we may regard certain things as fantastic

inventions, as, for instance, Lord Nonsuch and others in
Dryden's *Wild Gallant* believing themselves with child.
Yet with reference to this Genest quotes a story of a
' Dr. Pelling, Chaplain to Charles II, who having studied
himself into the disorder of mind called the hyp . . . between
the age of forty and fifty imagined himself to be pregnant '.

The same is true as regards scenes ; wherever they could,
the comic writers of this period took what they were able
from the life they saw around them. Dryden would never
have considered it a compliment to learn what Lamb may
have told him in Hades, and he wrote with pride of his
son's *Husband his own Cuckold* that ' the circumstances
really happened in Rome '. Cibber took his handkerchief
scene in *The Careless Husband* from real life, and, according
to Dennis, the story on which Shadwell's *Squire of Alsatia*
' was built was a true fact '.* Mock marriages also, so
frequent in these comedies, as, for instance, in *The Country
Wife*, had their part in reality, and were not devices invented for stage purposes. It is on record that the Earl of
Oxford carried out a sham ceremony with a famous actress
of impregnable virtue, probably Mrs. Marshall, who upon
appealing to the king got no further redress than some
monetary compensation.

The bargaining scene in *The Way of the World* has always
been considered the height of artificial comedy. Mirabell
lays down as a condition of marriage with Millamant that
at the tea-table ' you exceed not in your province ; but
restrain yourself to native and simple tea-table drinks, as tea,
chocolate and coffee. . . . I banish all foreign forces, all
auxiliaries to the tea-table, as orange brandy, all aniseed,
cinnamon, citron and Barbadoes waters.' Such an ' odious

* The main idea, however, is from the *Adelphœ* of Terence.

proviso' may seem extravagant to us, yet in a foot-note to
the Mermaid edition we read, ' With those beverages there
was always a mixture of alcohol. The poets and satirists
were very severe upon the " tasting " of fine ladies ', in
illustration of which a short passage is quoted. And in
Genest we find that in her room at court Miss Hobart
' had a cupboard stocked with comfits and all kinds of
liqueurs '.

To quote again from Genest upon another topic. ' The
character of Foresight (*Love for Love*) is now become obso-
lete . . . but in 1695 there could not be a more fair subject
for ridicule, as persons of the first ability were guilty of that
folly (astrology); Dryden, in a letter to his sons in Rome
written at this time, says: " Towards the latter end of
September Charles will begin to recover his perfect health,
according to his nativity, which casting it myself I am sure
is true, and all things hitherto have happened according to
the time that I predicted them." The famous Lord Shaftesbury, though as to religion a Deist, had in him the dotage
of astrology to a high degree—he said to Burnet that a
Dutch doctor had from the stars foretold him the whole
series of his life.' That the superstition was popular
enough we may gather from Rochester's prank as an astrologer; and how far it was accepted may be gauged from
the fact that the compiler of a medical book of the period
named himself ' Physician and Astrologer '. The theme of
the mock astrologer was used as early as Wilson's *The
Cheats* (1662), or, indeed, as Massinger's *City Madam*; and
as late as Farquhar's *Recruiting Officer* (1706).

The point need not be laboured. Enough has been quoted
to show that the general life of the time, its movement, its
amusements, its general conceptions, were mirrored upon
the stage. ' No one ', as Mr. Street writes, ' conversant

with the memoirs of the court can have any difficulty in matching the fiction with its reality.' And while it is true that this comedy, written moreover for the most part by men who had at least the aloofness necessary to art, need make no appeal to our passions, not to connect them ' in any shape with the result to be drawn from their imitation in real life ', is an error which can only be excused by the enthusiasm of a great artist who wished at all costs to save exquisite work from the oblivion to which an ignorant Grundyism would have consigned it. At the present day we can afford to be frank.

III

THE COMEDY OF MANNERS

Its Relation to the Comedy of Humours.

THE line of demarcation between the comedy of manners and the comedy of humours is none too clear. It consists partly in a difference in stagecraft rather than a difference of outlook, in a greater vivacity of rendering rather than a variation in profundity. Restoration comedy was much lighter in the handling of personalities, altogether more deft, than the comedy of humours. The moral did not have to be driven home with bludgeon blows, and the temper of a man could be appreciated without depicting the excesses of a Volpone or the madness of a Sir Giles Overreach.

It attacked the unsocial from another angle. Whereas the comedy of humours searched out and displayed the hidden recesses of human passions and desires, the comedy of manners showed that these passions and desires were by no means confined in hidden recesses, but might be encountered daily. Morose, set in an almost imaginary town, became Manly who was supposed to walk about the London everybody knew. The audience, instead of being asked to recognize something of themselves in the characters they saw upon the stage, were invited to laugh at their acquaintance. Finally, the comedy of humours was only more profound in that it appealed to some supposedly absolute standard of morality, while the comedy of manners took for its norm that of the *honnête homme* of the time.

This is not to say that Restoration comedy was less in earnest than the Elizabethan. In presenting characters familiar to every one, the exquisite in his Chedreux wig, the would-be wit, or the gay lady of fashion, it did not merely seek to amuse, and attract audiences by showing them fashionable life lived up to the hilt. It tried just as profoundly to reveal mankind and consider the effect of passions, but it dealt with everything more intellectually, more urbanely, more cynically perhaps. It was gayer, and did not take its wisdom with so desperate a seriousness; it was entirely without the metaphysical element. But if there was not so much *furor poeticus*, there was just as much considered criticism. For why were the figures put upon the stage if not for crushing ridicule? The dialogue was admittedly pointed, but at what? Wit cannot exist in the air; it is necessarily critical, or even satirical: it must be referred to something, and this something was what the comic writers of the period were pleased to call 'acquired follies'. Sir Fopling Flutter is the main figure of *The Man of Mode* because, in the words of Dorimant, ' he is a person of great acquired follies '. In the same manner Congreve, in *The Way of the World*, strove ' to design some characters which should appear ridiculous not so much through a natural folly . . . as through an affected wit '.

How ' acquired follies ' were to be recognized apart from the inborn is a question which does not seem to have occurred to many writers of that period. There is no immediately visible difference between an affectation and a vice, and Congreve's Scandal was right when he said there was ' no effectual difference between continued affectation and reality '; for although in the ' Letter concerning Humour ' Congreve defined the difference with great lucidity, the ' humour ' being ineradicable, the ' folly ' artificial, he gave no test by which the one could be distinguished from the other at a glance. Shadwell, who definitely hoped to continue the Jonsonian tradition, and was convinced that he wrote the comedy of humours, declared that he despised the 'farce-fools' whose humour was nothing more than extravagant dress, and that he aimed at the 'artificial folly of those who are not coxcombs by nature, but with great art and industry make themselves so', in fact the Jonsonian 'sporting' with 'follies not with crimes'. Vanbrugh has a passage to the same effect in *The Relapse*, where Loveless tells Amanda to 'pity those whom nature abuses, but never those who abuse nature'. But after all, the spring which moves people to abuse nature has been planted in them by nature herself.

In reality Congreve and Shadwell based their theory upon the induction to *Every Man Out of His Humour*.

> . . . Whatsoe'er hath fluxure and humidity,
> As wanting power to contain itself,
> Is humour. So in every human body,
> The choler, melancholy, phlegm and blood,
> By reason that they flow continually
> In some one part, and are not continent,
> Receive the name of Humours. Now thus far
> It may, by metaphor, apply itself
> Unto the general disposition;
> As when some one peculiar quality
> Doth so possess a man, that it doth draw
> All his affects, his spirits, and his powers,
> In their confluctions, all to run one way,
> This may be truly said to be a humour.
> But that a rook, by wearing a pied feather,
> The cable hat-band, or the three-piled ruff,
> A yard of shoe-tie, or the Switzer's knot
> On his French garters, should affect a humour!
> O, it is more than most ridiculous.

And let us remember here that Jonson also intended to 'strip the ragged follies *of the time*'.

Restoration comedy as often as not dealt with what Jonson himself would have called humours. Congreve's Captain Bluffe is only Bobadill's grandson, Witwoud is lineally sprung from Sir John Daw, while Sir Amorous Lafoole has a hundred descendants. The only difference is that after 1660 there was on the whole a greater variety, a brisker mingling, we might say a lighter hand. Yet Jonson himself could be light enough, as witness this passage from *Every Man in His Humour* (III. i):

> *Matthew.* Oh! it's your only fine humour, sir. Your true melancholy breeds your perfect fine wit, sir. I am melancholy myself, divers times, sir; and then do I no more but take pen and paper, presently, and overflow you half a score or a dozen of sonnets at a sitting. . . .
> *Stephen.* Truly, sir, and I love such things out of measure. . . .
> *Matthew.* Why, I pray you, sir, make use of my study; it's at your service.
> *Stephen.* I thank you, sir, I shall be so bold, I warrant you. Have you a stool there, to be melancholy upon?

Has it not got the very ring of a Restoration comedy? As an isolated passage one might easily guess it to belong to the later period.

In truth, Restoration writers themselves saw no vast unlikeness between the Jonsonian form and their own, and in the great majority of cases never got the difference in atmosphere clear. In the same way Massinger probably did not realize that *A City Madam* was in this matter something quite different from *A New Way to Pay Old Debts*. Only gradually do we see, not merely in each individual writer, but progressively throughout the period, steps being made towards a different method. Continually the humours blunder in upon the manners and spoil them; the heavy touch shatters the delicate effects. For if the actual point of divergence cannot be indicated, there is at

the extremes an evident difference between the two forms
of comedy. The method of the 'humour' comedy was
akin to that of the moralities, that is, to clothe some
abstract quality in the garb of a man, invest it with such
realistic trappings as to make it appear passably like a
human being, and set it amongst its fellows, the whole
relieved often, as was Jonson's way, against a background
taken from real life. It tried to be critical, not of its own
time but of humanity. It began with an attempted universality, leaving its immediate application to chance, or the
spectator's conscience. The comedy of manners applied an
inverse method. It was immediately critical, and in so far
as it aimed at universality, as any art worthy of the name
must do, it aimed at it through the individual. The comedy
of humours never attempted to paint the full man, moved
by inconsistencies, urged by conflicting passions, whereas,
in the main, the comedy of manners did ; and the passions
were by no means all on the superficial level of frills and
sword knots, repartee, and bawdy talk that is often taken
for granted as the characteristic note of Restoration
work.

The comedy of manners, then, was no exception to any
other critical comedy, and no class was spared by the
Restoration wits, who, not content with the 'acquired
follies' of their friends, flung their satirical net, not only
over the eastern portions of London, but over the country
seats that entrenched the savage Sir Tunbelly Clumseys,
and where maidens found pleasure in inhaling the fragrance
of those 'filthy nosegays'. Thus it was the immediate as
opposed to the enduring critical intent that developed the
comedy of manners out of the comedy of humours. Both,
in the hands of artists, became works of art whose didactic
message we can, if we wish, ignore.

Wit.

There is another point which distinguished the comedy of manners from that of humours, namely, the verbal pyrotechnics. These are at once its glory and its bane; the former because wit made for clarity of expression, the latter because the standard changes. By the quality of its wit Restoration comedy is immediately 'dated'; nor was it always of the highest kind. Much, indeed, is on the level of Swift's *Polite Conversation*. 'A penny for your thought.' 'It is not worth a farthing, for I was thinking of you', is no worse than much Restoration fencing. And even where it is good of its kind it often becomes tedious, the perpetual search for a simile very wearisome. The stiffness of manner we have sometimes to complain of in Wycherley is due, as Pope said, to 'his being always studying for antitheses'. Let us take a passage from the best of his plays, *The Country Wife* (I. i). Harcourt, Horner, and Dorilant are speaking of Sparkish :—

> *Horn.* . . . he 's one of those nauseous offerers at wit, who, like the worst fiddlers, run themselves into all companies.
>
> *Har.* One that, by being in the company of men of sense, would pass for one.
>
> *Horn.* And may so to the short-sighted world; as a false jewel among true ones is not discerned at a distance. His company is as troublesome to us as a cuckold's when you have a mind to his wife's.
>
> *Har.* No, the rogue will not let us enjoy one another, but ravishes our conversation; though he signifies no more to 't than Sir Martin Mar-all's gaping, and awkward thrumming on the lute, does to his man's voice and music.
>
> *Dor.* And to pass for a wit in town shows himself a fool every night to us, that are guilty of the plot.
>
> *Horn.* Such wits as he are, to a company of reasonable men, like rooks to the gamesters; who only fill a room at the table, but are so far from contributing to the play, that they only serve to spoil the fancy of those that do.

Dor. Nay, they are used like rooks too, snubbed, checked, and abused; yet the rogues will hang on.

Horn. A pox on 'em, and all that force nature, and would be still what she forbids 'em! Affectation is her greatest monster.

Har. Most men are the contraries to that they would seem. Your bully, you see, is a coward with a long sword; the little humbly-fawning physician, with his ebony cane, is he that destroys men.

Dor. The usurer, a poor rogue, possessed of mouldy bonds and mortgages; and we they call spendthrifts, are only wealthy, who lay out his money upon daily new purchases or pleasure.

Horn. Ay, your arrantest cheat is your trustee or executor; your jealous man the greatest cuckold; your churchman the greatest atheist; and your noisy pert rogue of wit the greatest fop, dullest ass, and worst company, as you shall see; for here he comes.

But again, this epigrammatic talk was part of the fashionable life of the day, and was constantly used by such men as Sir Charles Sedley, who, Etherege wrote from Ratisbon, would sometimes speak more wit at supper than was to be heard in any play.* That this was also the gallant's own opinion we learn from Pepys, who one day heard Sir Charles in the pit distract the delighted audience's attention from the dulness of the piece. Its failures, of course, provided comedy with much amusing material; and when Etherege, Wycherley, or Congreve show a would-be wit straining after a simile the concentrated effect of ridicule is highly diverting.

It is this persistent attempt to be witty that makes many people regard Restoration comedy as tedious, undramatic stuff, during the acting of which persons come upon the stage merely to fire off epigrams at one another. But this

* Shadwell paid him the same compliment in the dedication of *A True Widow.*

continual definition was only a part of the desire of the
men of that period to see themselves clearly; it was part
of their curiosity, of their attempt to rationalize. It was
also to some extent a desire to polish the surface of life; we
must remember that the Restoration age foreshadowed the
Augustan. No Dryden, no Pope. We may now and again
find the method tiresome, but it has its interest, and even
its beauty.

As an example of this type of criticism we may take
Mr. Archer's suggestion that the weakness of Restoration
comedy lies in the fact that it was written for a coterie, its
talk 'essentially coterie talk, keyed up to the pitch of a
particular and narrow set'. Comedy, he maintains, became
the 'introspection of the coterie'. This is true, but is it
relevant to our judgement of these comedies as works of
art? For the point is not whether they may have been
written for a coterie, but how great were the minds that
used the ideas and talk of the 'particular and narrow set'
as material for art. The distance between the subject and
the created thing cannot be measured. If Etherege did not
see beyond the life of his companions, Wycherley assuredly
did. If Vanbrugh took life as he found it, it is certain that
Congreve was far from doing so. The essential point is to
penetrate the attitude towards life, any life, brought by the
writers to the making of their works of art.

IV

ITS DESCENT

'WE waste our time and lose our way if we try to connect what we see (in Restoration comedy) with the productions of the Elizabethan age', says Mr. Gosse. Yet Swinburne spoke of 'the gap between Etherege and Fletcher, a bridge on which Shirley may shake hands with Shadwell, and Wycherley with Brome'. Here then is a clear issue: Was Restoration comedy an offshoot of the French theatre, or was it of English extraction? The matter is in one sense unimportant; but nevertheless a solution of the question may bring us nearer the works themselves, because in one case they are a natural growth, in the other an artificial thing stuck on, almost inevitably without depth. We will endeavour to see how far this comedy developed naturally from the late Elizabethan, and what exactly it owed to the French.

The subject-matter which characterizes Restoration comedy is to be found in the Elizabethan plays down to the closing of the theatres (1642). There, rather than in France, is the material to be found, besides that which was to be gleaned from the society of the day. Let us first take the important question of sex-antagonism, revealing itself in a dislike for marriage, the defence of young women against ardent besiegers, and the desire of married women and widows to take their freedom and preserve their 'honour' or their independence.

The English note against marriage was sounded on the stage as early as *The First Shepherd's play* (c. 1425), where

we read ' We silly wed-men dree mickle woe ' ; * though
it was not until well into the Shakespearian age that we
find the theme developed. But already in Marston's *Dutch
Courtezan* we get some very advanced passages, of which
we may quote one here as being of especial interest.

> *Beatrice.* My love here.
> *Crispinella.* Prithee call him not love, 'tis the drab's phrase ;
> nor sweet honey, nor my coney, nor dear duckling, 'tis the
> citizen's terms, but call him——
> *Beatrice.* What ?
> *Crispinella.* Anything.

Let us now compare this with the famous passage from *The
Way of the World*, ' an exquisite passage ', Mr. Palmer says,
' beyond which the comedy of manners has never in any
language reached '.

> *Millamant.* I won't be called names after I'm married ; posi-
> tively I won't be called names.
> *Mirabell.* Names !
> *Millamant.* Ay, as wife, spouse, my dear, joy, jewel, love,
> sweetheart, and the rest of that nauseous cant, in which men
> and their wives are so fulsomely familiar.

Congreve's passage is far superior in style and feeling, but
not very different in idea or treatment. Does not Crispinella as much as Millamant voice the ideal of being
' very strange and well-bred ' ? And surely Congreve got his
idea of the bargain scene from Massinger's *The City Madam*,
where Sir Maurice Lacy asks for the hand of Anne Frugal.

> *Anne.*   I require first,—
> And that, since 'tis in fashion with kind husbands,
> In civil manners you must grant,—my will
> In all things whatsoever, and that will
> To be obeyed, not argued . . .
> . . . having my page, my gentleman usher,
> My woman sworn to my secrets, my caroch. . . .

and so on for some twenty lines.

* *Towneley Plays*, ed. England and Pollard (E.E.T.S.), p. 118.

But Marston's Crispinella is some fifty years in front of
her time, as when she says :

> A husband generally is a careless, domineering thing, that
> grows like coral, which as long as it is under water is soft and
> tender, but as soon as it has got its branch above the waves is
> presently hard, stiff, not to be bowed but burst; so that when
> a husband is a suitor and under your choice, Lord how supple
> he is, how obsequious, how at your service, sweet lady . . .

speaking and thinking like any Restoration young woman.
Thus Bellmour says to Belinda in Congreve's *The Old
Bachelor* :

> But you timorous virgins form a dreadful chimera of a
> husband, as of a creature contrary to that soft, humble, pliant,
> easy thing, a lover.

The phraseology is hardly different; the variation is in
prose style rather than in anything else. And when Crispinella says :

> Pish ! sister Beatrice ; prithee read no more. My stomach of
> late stands against kissing extremely. By the faith and trust
> I bear to my face, 'tis grown one of the most unsavoury cere-
> monies ; body o' beauty ! 'Tis one of the most unpleasing,
> injurious customs to ladies,

she is by no means unlike a Restoration lady, with the
typical ' coldness ', which if not always real was frequently
feigned.

If with Shakespeare and Fletcher, and even Jonson to
the very end of the period, marriage is the happy haven for
lovers, the Restoration flavour was not lacking long before
the great rebellion. If we have only hints in such early
plays as Marston's and Middleton's, in Brome and Shirley
it has become very definite. The tedium of the marriage
state is referred to implicitly and explicitly. In Brome's
Sparagus Garden, Rebecca, dissatisfied with her husband,
says, ' I see whatsoever shift a woman makes with her

husband at home, a friend does best abroad'; and in his *Mad Couple Well Match'd*, Careless in a letter talks of 'escaping the captivity of matrimony'. In Shirley's *The Lady of Pleasure* Sir Thomas Bornwell says to his wife, in counterfeit certainly, but it was possible to say it:

> I must
> Acknowledge 't was thy care to disenchant me
> From a dull husband to an active lover,

and in his *Witty Fair One* people 'commit' matrimony with a sneer as obvious as any in Wycherley or Congreve.

In *The Parson's Wedding* (printed 1663, but probably written when Killigrew was abroad, before the Restoration) we read:

> *Widow.* Fie, Captain, repent for shame, and marry.
> *Capt.* Your ladyship would have said marry and repent: no, though it be not the greatest pleasure, yet it is better than marrying, for when I am weary of her, my inconstancy is termed virtue, and I shall be said to turn to grace. Beware of women for better for worse, for our wicked nature, when her sport is lawful, cloys straight; therefore rather than marry, keep a wench.

This is pure Restoration style, the appeal to 'our wicked nature' is Etherege all over. But does it sound more like Molière, or Middleton, Shirley, and Brome? * Indeed the theme of sex-antagonism is almost completely absent from French comedy.

The Material.

If the attitude towards love and marriage, as treated by the Restoration writers, was no new thing in our literature, in *The Wits* by D'Avenant, as in many others (such as *The Lady of Pleasure*), the fashionable life of the time

* One might also point to the Clown's remarks in *All 's Well that Ends Well*, I. iii.

also begins to be portrayed, and we have the country boor and country life derided by the ladies of fashion. The conversation between the Elder Palatine, Lady Ample, Lucy, and Sir Morglay Thwack may serve as an example:

> *Lucy.* Pray how do the ladies there? Poor villagers
> They churn still, keep their dairies, and lay up
> For embroidered mantles, against the heir's birth . . .
> *Thwack.* Poor country Madams, th' are in subject still,
> The beasts their husbands make 'em sit on three
> Legg'd stools, like homely daughters of an hospital
> To knit socks for their cloven feet. . . .
> *Lucy.* And then the evenings (warrant ye) they spend
> With mother Spectacle the curate's wife,
> Who does inveigh 'gainst curling and dyed cheeks,
> Heaves her devout impatient nose at oil
> Of Jessamin, and thinks powder of Paris more
> Profane than th' ashes of a Roman martyr.
> *Lady Ample.*   They do frisk and dance
> In narrow parlours to a single fiddle
> That squeaks forth tunes, like a departing pig.

The theme occurs in almost any Restoration comedy, an attitude made fun of most deliciously by Dryden; but it is Harriet in *The Man of Mode* who expresses it most beautifully, for Etherege had too much sympathy to satirize, and was ever a poet. Harriet bewails her enforced return to

> a great rambling lone house that looks as it were not inhabited, the family's so small; there you'll find my mother, an old lame aunt, and myself, sir, perched up on chairs at a distance in a large parlour, sitting moping like three or four melancholy birds in a spacious volery. . . . Methinks I hear the hateful noise of rooks already—knaw, knaw, knaw. There's music in the worst cry in London.

Certainly, as far as general movement is concerned, the Restoration writers of comedy did not need to cross the Channel to bring realism and everyday life on to the stage. It is once more Shirley and Brome who lead the way. The former's *Hyde Park*, as Mr. Gosse concedes, ' is

unusually interesting as a study of contemporary manners ',
and indeed the open-air life of bustle, the pursuit of ladies
by gentlemen, the unexpected meetings in the walks of
Hyde Park amid the cries of outer life, are clear anticipa-
tions of the passages in St. James's Park or The Mall we
find in Sedley, Etherege, Wycherley, and Congreve. In
Brome's *Sparagus Garden* we have any of the pleasure-garden
scenes of thirty and forty years later; ladies with their
gallants; drinking, observation, and wit; and moreover we
have a formal dance introduced for its own sake, as with
Etherege or Dryden. Here also a great point is made of
the Sedan chair which had just been introduced, just as
during the Restoration period the latest novelty in the
streets was brought upon the stage.

The earlier work, indeed, is full of naturalistic touches.
Even in *A Match at Midnight* we get the widow saying,
' Pray go to Aldgate to my sempstress, for my ruff. Did
you bid her hollow it out just in the French fashion cut ? '
And in Jasper Mayne's *The City Match* (printed 1639) we read:

> Gentlemen,
> Shall we dine at the ordinary ? You
> Shall enter me among the wits,

and we need not again call attention to *The City Madam*.
If, as is said, the Restoration stage owed its ' increasing
naturalness ' to *Les Précieuses Ridicules*, to what, we may
ask, was due the ' increasing naturalness ' of Massinger,
Shirley, and Brome ?

Further, as manners go, in the linking period between
Shirley and Etherege, Cockain's Lorece, when he is wooing
Vandora is surely speaking to a Restoration woman in
promising that when he marries her

> I at any time will carry you to a play, either to the Black
> Friars or Cockpit. And you shall go to the Exchange when

you will, and have as much money as you please to lay out
You shall find me a very loving husband, in truth, dear lady.

We cannot but be reminded of this passage when we hear
Wycherley's Gerrard promising Hippolita that when he
marries her he would ' carry ' her ' to Court, the play-
houses, and 'Hyde Park '.

To return, however, to Shirley. In more ways than one
he anticipated the later period, and perhaps his Frederick
may claim to be the ancestor of the prevailing party of fops
and coxcombs, the forbear of Sir Fopling Flutter, Sir
Courtly Nice, Selfish, and Lord Foppington. ' How d'you
like me now ? ' he asks his steward. ' Most excellent ', he
is answered. Thereupon he turns to another. ' Your opinion,
Master Littleworth ', and is told, ' Your French tailor has
made you a perfect gentleman ', and so on for some forty
lines.

But if any play of the pre-rebellion period can claim to
be the first play in the Restoration manner, it is, as Swinburne suggested, Brome's *Mad Couple*. There can be no
doubt but that Wycherley and Congreve were well acquainted with this play, and perhaps Etherege. Mrs. Behn
made it the foundation of her *Debauchee*. As far as movement goes it is not unlike *She Would if She Could*, and
Etherege may have taken from thence his scene in the
mercer's shop. These, however, are vague statements ; the
close acquaintance can be better substantiated by examples.

We may take first the Fidelia portions of Wycherley's
Plain Dealer. It is usually said that Fidelia is an adaptation
of Viola in *Twelfth Night* ; or that she comes from Fletcher's *Philaster*, by way, perhaps, of Cockain's *Obstinate
Lady*. But in the above cases, although there are naturally
many resemblances in the treatment of a theme popular
ever since Barnaby Rich published his tale in 1581, there

is not the agreement in detail. Wycherley's plot is more ingenious, the unravelling more exciting, but so closely are the incidents followed that it is difficult to believe that he did not base himself upon the earlier play.

Congreve also was well acquainted with Brome, and it is possible that Vainlove who 'quits an amour where others take it up', was developed and infinitely subtilized from Sir Arnold Cautious in *Sparagus Garden*, 'an infinite admirer of beauty but dares not touch a woman'. According to Genest, 'Congreve in *The Old Bachelor* has borrowed the characters of Sir Joseph Wittol and Captain Bluffe from Widgine and Anvil', in Brome's *Northern Lass*, which was revived in 1684. But his debt to *A Mad Couple* is more evident than in the instances we have noted. Careless's talk about his aunt, his love-making to her in spite of the danger of a consequent heir to disinherit him, although different in development, is too like Mellefont's relationship with his aunt, Lady Touchwood (*The Double Dealer*), to allow us to think that Congreve had here invented or imported something that did not already exist in the English drama. Further, there is one passage which seems to be deliberate borrowing. Brome's Lady Thrivewell is accusing her husband of infidelity:

> *Thrive.* How can you think so?
> *Lady T.* I see it apparently upon your face, and hear it in your sighs. Your broken sleep to-night when your own groans waked you declared no less . . . once you took me in your arms, but when you found out 'twas I, you turn'd away as in a dream.

Congreve adapts this as follows in *The Old Bachelor*. Araminta accuses Belinda, the man-hater, of being in love:

> *Aramin.* You don't know that you dreamed of Bellmour last night, and called him aloud in your sleep.

Belin. Pish! I can't help dreaming of the Devil sometimes; would you from thence infer I love him?

Aramin. But that's not all; you caught me in your arms when you named him, and pressed me to your bosom. Sure, if I had not pinched you till you waked, you had stifled me with kisses.

It is very easy to urge this kind of relationship to absurd extremes, and we could quote a couplet from Congreve's *The Mourning Bride* not unlike one to be found in this play of Brome's. But the point is not to prove plagiarism so much as a general likeness, and Congreve, as a matter of fact, is full of reminiscences of the older writers.

It would be easy to multiply instances; for example, we might give Zanche's dream in *The White Devil* and Prue's dream in *The Gentleman Dancing Master*, which are both related for the same purpose, and are both, well—Freudian. But enough has been said to show that Restoration comedy can claim legitimate descent from our own earlier plays.

French Plots in English Comedy.

The fact that English comedy from the early years of the Restoration until well into the eighteenth century abounds with French plots has led people to think that our stage was thereby influenced. This is very doubtful. Our writers, like Molière himself, took their good things where they could find them, from Latin, Spanish, and French sources, but above all from the life around them. For although there are close translations as well as free adaptations from Molière, Regnard, Boursault, and others, these always maintain the standpoint, the form, and the atmosphere, of English comedy, that is to say, the essential things that distinguish one work of art from another. Even in frank translations, such as Vanbrugh's *Confederacy* from the *Bourgeoises à la Mode* of Dancourt, something that is French has been lost, much that is unmistakably English has been added. Mr. Whibley, writing of *The Confederacy*, says: 'Closely as it follows the original, it is racy of our soil. As you read it, you think not of the French original, but of Middleton and Dekker. It was as though Vanbrugh had breathed an English soul into a French body.' That this is strictly true we may illustrate from a passage which indicates how Vanbrugh achieved this result. Any scene might be taken, but the shortness of this one commends it. Dancourt had written:

> *Jasmin.* Madame Amelin, votre marchande de modes . . .
> *Lisette.* C'est de l'argent qu'elle vous demande.
> *Angel.* Je n'en ai point à lui donner.

In Vanbrugh's hands this becomes:

> *Jessamin.* Madam, there 's the woman below that sells paints and patches iron-bodice, false teeth, and all sorts of things to the ladies: I can't think of her name.
> *Flippanta.* 'Tis Mrs. Amlet; she wants money.
> *Clarissa.* Well, I han't enough for myself; it 's an unreasonable thing she should think I have any for her.

The difference is startling, for the object of French comedy was something quite different from that of the English. The former aimed at atmosphere, the latter at acute characterization and high-flavoured speech. A French valet might indulge in images, and even quote Racine, an English one had to confine himself to the vernacular of his class.

French comedy aimed at an aesthetic result, English comedy at being amusingly moral; the first at wisdom, the wisdom of the artist read between the lines, the second at a direct didacticism and a homely setting. In this connexion we may profitably compare Molière's *Amphitryon* with that of Dryden: the latter might have called forth the guffaws of Squire Western, the former was a wise and delicate fantasy that would have been far above his head. Sosie dilated upon the fears of night travelling, but would never have said, as did Sosia, ' Lord, how am I melted into sweat with fear : I am diminished of my natural weight above two stone : I shall not bring half myself home again to my poor wife and family '.

This indicates that the atmosphere, the only really important influence, would not suffer the sea voyage. As a rule the English could not forbear pointing the moral ; the curse of the humours nearly always threatened any structure that aimed at being purely poetic. Again, the English never left anything to the imagination. Just as in a previously quoted passage the French were content to know a *marchande de modes* was at the door, while we English had to be told the exact scope of her activities, so in Regnard's *Gamester* we never see the hero at play, whereas Mrs. Centlivre in her adaptation gives us a scene with the hero, his leader in vice, and ' several rakes and sharpers ' who play a whole game out in front of us. In this country we always needed the physical counterpart of the words, which by themselves were not enough. The French were content with suggestions to wing the imagination ; we have always been brass-tackers. Thus it was that when the Restoration comedy writers adopted French plots they transformed them beyond recognition.

Molière provides the most evident examples. ' In his plays ', Taine remarks (justly, if we omit his farces), ' there is no complication, no incidents. One comic event suffices for the story. A dozen conversations make up the play of *Le Misanthrope*.' But when Alceste becomes Manly in *The Plain Dealer*, he is not an ordinary member of the society in which he moves, but a sailor, which at once makes a difference in the angle of criticism. And, besides this, the whole construction is different, two other plots, one extremely romantic and Fletcherian, being introduced. But to make clear this point of flesh and blood actuality, we may remember that in *Le Misanthrope* we hear that Alceste suffers from legal injustice. This, perhaps, gave Wycherley the idea of exposing the whole legal profession, and there are many scenes devoted to this subject. To accomplish his purpose Wycherley had to take an additional set of characters, but he did not engraft the Comtesse de Pimbèche from Racine, as is often stated, with small regard to the probable date of the first draft of *The Plain Dealer*. Just as Wilson had done in his purely Jonsonian play of *The Cheats* (1662), he adopted the generic lady of legal exposition, turning Abigail, ' a feme sole, seised in tail of the manor of Blackacre', into the Widow Blackacre, concerned with the fact that ' Ayle is seised in fee of Blackacre'. He could not, like Molière, leave it as a suggestion, for everything had to be driven in with blows of a maul, and no intelligence in the audience was taken for granted.

To take a plot, to borrow a subject, does not constitute influence, as we may see by Shadwell's adaptation of *Les Fâcheux* as *The Sullen Lovers*, or Dryden's *Sir Martin Mar-All* taken from *L'Étourdi*. In each case the plot had to be at least doubled. Indeed, Molière was always ' improved ' for our stage, which, as Dryden phrased it, was ' incomparably more curious in all the ornaments of Dramatic Poesy than the French or Spanish '. Downes remarked of *Sir Martin Mar-All* that Dryden had drawn it from a rough translation, ' curiously polishing the whole'. When Medbourne, an insignificant and now forgotten playwright, wrote a version of *Le Tartufe*, it was described as ' written in French by Molière, and rendered into English with much addition and advantage', an opinion which no doubt corresponded to the general taste. Such stuff was indeed, to use Pope's line, 'the frippery of crucified Molière'. So negligible did the great Frenchman's plays seem to many of our authors (though not to Dryden) that they scarcely acknowledged the most obvious debt to him. They felt they owed none. This was not necessarily because they thought they had greater minds, but because they thought his plays lacking in the requisites of liveliness and journalistic realism demanded by English audiences; in which, no doubt, they were right.

English plays, therefore, never aimed at producing the same cool atmosphere as the French. Not only were the whole scheme and scope utterly different, the very manner and attitude had no connexion with theirs. The English of those days did not paint broadly, they filled in with deft touches. All, from Etherege and Shadwell to Farquhar and Cibber, were inimitable observers of conversation, of gestures, of the superficies of manners. They could seize a man's character from the cut of his coat, or detect a woman's failing from the fall of a bodkin. They pounced immediately upon any mannerism that could be made at all ridiculous, any situation that promised fun, without bothering overmuch about the philosophic application. What they took from the French they spoiled; what they had in naturalness was, one may readily suppose, but the natural reflection of a life that was free, a result of a realism they could not avoid.

The Real Influence.

That there was a difference between the comedy of 1630 and that of 1670 cannot be denied. The latter was written not only for, but by a different set of people. Etherege was a typical gallant of his time, Wycherley a court favourite, Congreve the greatest wit in fashionable society. Peers entered the lists as competitors for the bays. Will's tavern, if not Whitehall itself, had replaced the *Mermaid*. The court and the theatre were on visiting, even marrying, terms. A greater delicacy in style, if not in manners, was made possible by the fact that, owing to the class from which its writers sprang, the great majority of the characters were ladies and gentlemen, and not citizens or boors as was often the case in Elizabethan comedy; and this was further increased by the final acceptance of women upon the stage, an experiment which in earlier days had wrought Prynne to fury. Also, for the first time, the capital became the definite centre of educated society. Life moved more briskly, and even more dangerously. The most had to be made of every moment, and at first there was no time to make profound philosophic generalizations. Thus the plays of Etherege are to those of Jonson what the little Tanagra figures are to the sculptures of Luxor. But the chief difference is in prose style.

Metaphor and simile became altogether less involved, and if in feeling and outlook, in the choice of imagery and wealth of fancy, our poets remained thoroughly English, they became more simple. We may take as examples two pieces of poetry transformed by Etherege and Congreve into the language of comedy. The first is from *Samson Agonistes*, and is of Dalila :

> That so bedeckt, ornate and gay,
> Comes this way, sailing
> Like a stately ship
> Of Tarsus, bound for the isles
> Of Javan or Gadire,
> With all her bravery on, and tackle trim,
> Sails fill'd, and streamers waving. . . .

It is in the grand manner; for the purpose of our writers

of comedy overweighted with allusion. They care nothing
for Javan or Gadire, but they are none the less poets, sure
of their mark, impelled by fancy rather than by imagination.
So Etherege wrote of Mistress Gatty :

> Tune her a jig and play't roundly, you shall see her bounce
> it away like a nimble frigate before a fresh gale—hey, methinks
> I see her under sail already.

Congreve did not better this in his description of Millamant's entry ; he could not avoid the satirical touch :

> Here she comes i' faith full sail, with her fan spread and
> streamers out, and a shoal of fools for tenders.

There is nothing foreign here.

Etherege's ' poetry ' is English. He may have learned
something in neatness from the French, but no more. His
rhymed couplets in *Love in a Tub* are scarcely better than
the blank verse of Brome and D'Avenant. The cadenced
melody of Molière's verse, the charm of an artificiality
which serves but to point the reality while softening the
realism, is foreign to the English method. Etherege's
couplets have, somehow, a faint flavour of the French
grace, but they could only serve him for the etiolated
romantic, and not the realistic, comedy. He could no more
have treated themes like *Le Menteur* or *Les Plaideurs* in
verse than he could have turned Puritan. When he wrote :

> *Aurelia.* Oh, no ; Heaven has decreed alas ! that we
> Should in our fates, not in our loves agree.
> *Bruce.* Dear friend, my rashness I too late repent ;
> I ne'er thought death till now a punishment,

he was writing bad French verse. But when he described
Harriet as having ' pretty pouting lips, with a little moisture
ever hanging on them, that look like the Provence rose
fresh on the bush, ere the morning sun has quite drawn up

the dew ', he was writing good English poetry, of a sort
Herrick would have appreciated. But it was not Elizabethan,
it was felt in quite a different manner, as an immediate
reaction to something delightful. There was nothing pondered about it. The difference is at once apparent if we
refer back to Middleton on the same theme:

> Upon those lips, the sweet fresh buds of youth,
> The holy dew of prayer lies, like a pearl
> Dropt from the opening eyelids of the morn
> Upon a bashful rose.

There is an easy grace about the courtier; as in the ship
simile, he did not wish to burden the clear comparison with
extraneous imagery. The tortuous euphuism, the metaphysical element, from which the Elizabethans never quite
shook themselves free, would have trammelled Etherege
too much. He certainly cared nothing for the holy dew of
prayer, and it would not occur to him that a rose might
be bashful. A dewdrop on the rose was a simple dewdrop
to him, and might or might not be like a pearl! It was no
concern of his. The sun might suck up the dew, that was
a matter of observation, but, for him, the morn would
never have eyelids to open.

We may say, in fact, that it was French life rather than
French literary form that was reflected in our comedies
through the medium of the court, in confirmation of which
we may appeal to Dryden. In his dedication of *Marriage
à la Mode* to Rochester, he said, ' And not only I, who
pretend not this way, but the best Comick Writers of
our Age, will join with me to acknowledge, that they have
copied the Gallantries of Courts, the Delicacy of Expression, and the Decencies of Behaviour, from Your Lordship,
with more Success, than if they had taken their Models
from the Court of *France* '. For what happened was that

' society' had learned to talk, and it was here that the French influence was felt, not as imitation of dramatic form, but as improved social skill. Dryden was emphatic on this point in the *Defence of the Epilogue*, and claimed that the greater readiness in repartee in the comedies of his time as compared with those of the Jacobeans was due to this. In the Epilogue to the second part of the *Conquest of Granada* he wrote, with reference to Jonson's plays :

> Wit's now arrived to a more high degree,
> Our native Language more refin'd and free.
> Our Ladies and our Men now speak more Wit,
> In Conversation, than those poets writ.

The older poets, he argued, for all their ability could not have done what the men of his day were doing, simply because the material did not exist. Thus, although the importance of style in all things was more generally recognized, our writers remained English, and used to the full, unalloyed by French simplicity, their capacity for meticulous observation, direct simile, and all the wealth of bursting vitality that was their inalienable heritage from the earlier years of their century. The only important influence was linguistic.

And the reform, perhaps unfortunate, as involving a shrinkage of vocabulary, was deliberate, as is clear enough from Dryden's Epistle Dedicatory of *Troilus and Cressida*. ' But how barbarously we yet write and speak, your Lordship knows, and I am sufficiently sensible in my own *English*. For I am often put to a stand, in considering whether what I write be the Idiom of the Tongue, or false *Grammar*, and Nonsense couched beneath that specious Name of *Anglicism*. And have no other way to clear my Doubts, but by translating my *English* into *Latin*, and thereby trying what Sense the Words will bear in a more stable Language. I am desirous, if it were possible, that we might all write with the same Certainty of Words, and Purity of Phrase, to which the *Italians* first arrived, and after them the *French*: At least that we might advance so far, as our Tongue is capable of such a Standard.'

That in this respect the stage as a whole was to some extent affected cannot be doubted. Dryden, notoriously, was an eager student of Corneille; not only are there resemblances in the plays, but there is a close relation, either of agreement or dissent, between the *Essay of Dramatic Poesy* and *Trois Discours sur la Poésie Dramatique*. Perhaps also the king's wishes had some small influence. The Earl of Orrery says in a letter to one of his friends: 'I have now finished a play in the French manner; because I heard the King declare himself more in favour of their way of writing than of ours.' Again, St. Évremond, writing to Corneille, said: 'Mr. Waller, one of the finest minds of the century, is always eager to see your new plays, and does not fail to translate one or two acts into English verse for his own satisfaction.' The influence, as far as it went, was reflected rather in tragedy, with which we are not here concerned, yet it may be instructive to note that the one writer in that field who appears to us to excel his fellows is Otway, who undoubtedly wrote in the Elizabethan tradition,* although the plots of *Don Carlos* and *Venice Preserved* were taken from the Abbé Saint-Réal. Otway's was the natural English method, which was bound to triumph in its own country. Even Dryden, after some years, abandoned the attempt to develop along French lines, though he never lost the idea of classical construction that he held in common with the French. Such influence as there was in the use of the heroic couplet was short lived. Etherege,

* In spite of the rhymed couplets of *Don Carlos*.

who was influenced in this minor respect, threw it off after his first play, and Dryden only once used it, and that sparingly, for comedy.

The whole situation is admirably described by Pope in his *Epistle to Augustus* :

> Late, very late, correctness grew our care,
> When the tir'd nation breath'd from civil war.
> Exact Racine, and Corneille's noble fire,
> Show'd us that France had something to admire.
> Not but the tragic spirit was our own,
> And full in Shakespeare, fair in Otway shone :
> But Otway fail'd to polish or refine,
> And fluent Shakespeare scarce effac'd a line.
> Even copious Dryden wanted, or forgot,
> The last and greatest art, the art to blot.
>   Some doubt if equal pains, or equal fire
> The humbler muse of comedy require.
> But in known images of life, I guess
> The labour greater, as the indulgence less.
> Observe how seldom e'en the best succeed :
> Tell me if Congreve's fools are fools indeed ?
> What pert, low dialogue has Farquhar writ !
> How Van wants grace, who never wanted wit ! . . .
> And idle Cibber, how he breaks the laws,
> To make poor Pinky eat with vast applause !

It seems fair to say then that Restoration comedy was of English growth, that it would have existed substantially the same had Molière never lived, and our own theatres never been closed because stage-plays were ' spectacles of pleasure, too commonly expressing lascivious mirth and levity '. And it is necessary to realize this, because if we approach these plays from the French angle, we shall, like Pope, find them sadly wanting. But if we regard them as a natural development, we shall meet in them much of the stir, and not a little of the overbrimming vitality we get in the Elizabethans themselves.

V

ETHEREGE (? 1635–91)

* *Love in a Tub*, 1664.
  She Would if She Could, 1668.
  The Man of Mode, 1676.

'*The air rarefied and pure, danger near, and the spirit full of a gay wickedness : these agree well together.*'—ZARATHUSTRA.

SEEN through the haze of time, Etherege appears as a brilliant butterfly, alighting only upon such things as attract him ; a creature without much depth, but of an extraordinary charm and a marvellous surety of touch.

He was professedly no student. 'The more necessary part of philosophy', he once wrote to Dryden, ' is to be learn'd in the wide world more than in the gardens of Epicurus' ; and again, to Lord Dover, 'The life I have led has afforded me little time to turn over books ; but I have had leisure sufficient, while I idly rolled about the town, to look into myself'. What he found in himself was that he was infinitely delighted in the delicate surface of things, and that not for the world would he have had anything changed. All was entertaining to ' gentle George ' or ' easy Etherege ', to that ' loose wand'ring Etherege, in wild pleasures tost ', of whom Southern wrote. All, except hard work.

Thus his is a perfectly simple, understandable figure in Restoration court society ; he is in tune with it. His friends were Buckingham, Sedley, Rochester, Buckhurst—

---

* These lists are not all complete. Where the output was big only the most important plays are given.

with the last of whom he 'carried the two draggle-tailed nymphs one bitter frosty night over the Thames to Lambeth'*—and, above all, Dryden. He was the intimate of lords and wits, of actors (perhaps he used to spend musical evenings with the Bettertons) and of actresses. It was said he had a daughter by Mrs. Barry. He had friends at the *Rose*, and there was a lily at the *Bar*, for he was never absent from a new play, nor behindhand with a pretty woman.

Between his last two comedies he went on some diplomatic mission to Constantinople ;

> Ovid to Pontus sent for too much wit,
> Etherege to Turkey for the want of it,

they said. When he came back he resumed his gay life, rioted at Epsom with Rochester, and wrote his best play. Then he married for money so as to get a knighthood, or got a knighthood so as to marry for money, which it was is not quite clear. In any case he does not appear to have been fortunate :

> What then can Etherege urge in his defence,
> What reason bring, unless 'tis want of sense.
> For all he pleads beside is mere pretence . . .
> Merit with honour joined a crown to life,
> But he got honour for to get a wife.
> Preposterous knighthood! in the gift severe,
> For never was a knighthood bought so dear.

Etherege apparently agreed, for when in the year 1685 he was sent as envoy to Ratisbon, he left Dame Etherege behind. One of his letters to her remains :

I beg your pardon for undertaking to advise you. I am so well satisfied by your last letter of your prudence and judgement that I shall never more commit the same error. I wish there

---

* An episode of which he reminded Dorset in a letter from Ratisbon. Etherege, Letter-book, Brit. Mus. MS.

were copies of it in London; it might serve as a pattern for modest wives to write to their husbands. You shall find me so careful hereafter how I offend, you, that I will no more subscribe myself your loving since you take it ill, but

Madame,

Your most dutiful husband, G. E.

We see that he liked things to be clear cut.

And if he is perfectly simple to understand, so are his plays. They are pure works of art directed to no end but themselves, meant only, in Dryden's phrase, ' to give delight '. For Etherege was not animated by any moral stimulus, and his comedies arose from a superabundance of animal energy that only bore fruit in freedom and ease, amid the graces of Carolingian society. He was a hothouse product, and knew it. ' I must confess ', he once wrote, ' I am a fop in my heart. I have been so used to affectation, that without the help of the air of the court, what is natural cannot touch me.' So what was the use of Dryden urging him to ' scribble faster ' when he was abroad ? ' I wear flannel, sir,' he wrote to another friend, ' wherefore, pray, talk to me no more of poetry ', for his comedy was a gesture not very different in impulse from the exquisite tying of his cravat, or the set of his wig ; ' poetry ' to him was essentially an affair of silks and perfumes, of clavichord music and corrants.

His plays then are lyrical, in the sense of being immediate reactions to things seen around him, pondered only as works of art and not as expositions of views. He was a true naïf, ' too lazy and too careless to be ambitious ', as he wrote to Godolphin. He had no ethic to urge him to produce the laughter of social protection. His laughter, on the contrary, is always that of delight at being very much alive in the best of all possible societies, and is only corrective, here and there, by accident. There was, for

instance, no move in the sometimes graceful sex-game he
did not enjoy. 'Next to the coming to a good understanding with a new mistress', says Dorimant, whom, we may
remember, he perhaps designed as a portrait of himself,
' I love a quarrel with an old one; but the Devil 's in it,
there has been such a calm in my affairs of late, I have not
had the pleasure of making a woman break her fan, to be
sullen, or forswear herself these three days.' Or again, in
the words of Courtal, ' A single intrigue in love is as dull
as a single plot in a play, and will tire a lover worse than
t'other does an audience'. The motto of life is gaiety at
all costs, the first duty the defeat of dulness.

Indeed, there is no lack of plots in his first play; there
are no less than four—and a curious mixture they are.
There is a romantic Fletcherian plot, that of Lord Beau-
fort and Graciana, Bruce and Aurelia, written in rhymed
couplets ; a Middletonian one, with cheats and gamesters,
and a great deal of noise and drinking; a number of completely farcical scenes centring about the French valet Dufoy;
and finally the Sir Frederick-Widow tale, which, from
both the historical and artistic points of view is the most
interesting. It set the whole tone of Restoration comedy,
and gave out the chief theme, which was never relinquished.
At his first trial, with amazing intuition, Etherege had
laid his finger upon the most promising material of his
time.

The Comical Revenge, or Love in a Tub need not be taken
very seriously. It is on the whole a sheer ebullience of high
spirits, full of joyous pranks, practical joking, and charming
but not very real sentiment, in which the shrewd witty
observer of the later plays is almost entirely absent. Yet
his alertness for a telling simile, or for bringing all London
upon the stage, is apparent in the first act.

> *Lord Beaufort.* How now, cousin! What, at wars with the women?
>
> *Sir Frederick.* I gave a small alarm to their quarters last night, my lord.
>
> *Lord Beaufort.* Jenny in tears! What's the occasion, poor girl?
>
> *Maid.* I'll tell you, my lord.
>
> *Sir Frederick.* Buzz; set not her tongue going again (*clapping his hand before her mouth*). She has made more noise than half a dozen paper mills! London Bridge at low water is silence to her.

This is clever drawing, but most of this comedy is the purest tomfoolery. The valet, while drugged, is locked in a tub which he has to carry about on his shoulders. 'Vat aré you?' he cries, as he awakes. 'Jernie! Vat is dis? Am I Jack in a boxé? Begar, who did putté me here?' Disguise is the order of the day, and there is high-spirited burlesque, as when Sir Frederick dresses up his fiddlers as bailiffs, and Dufoy, released from his tub, thinks his master is in danger. He enters, therefore, 'with a helmet on his head, and a great sword in his hand, "Vare are de bougres de bailié! Tête-bleu, bougres rogues "', he cries, and 'falls upon the fiddlers'.

This is not comedy, but roaring, rollicking farce—that is, the fun depends upon incident. Our author had not found himself; there was small promise in all this of what was to come, little of the 'sense, judgement, and wit' for which Rochester was later to praise him. Yet in the Sir Frederick-Widow plot there are portions that treat most deliciously of the duel of the sexes.

> *Sir F.* Widow, I dare not venture myself in those amorous shades [of the garden]; you have a mind to be talking of love, I perceive, and my heart's too tender to be trusted with such conversation.
>
> *Widow.* I did not imagine you were so foolishly conceited; is it your wit or your person, sir, that is so taking?

Isn't it delightfully boy and girl?   And later:

> *Sir F.* By those lips,——
>
> *Widow.* Nay, pray forbear, sir——
>
> *Sir F.* Who is conceited now, widow?   Could you imagine I was so fond to kiss them?
>
> *Widow.* You cannot blame me for standing on my guard, so near an enemy. . . .
>
> *Sir F.* Let us join hands then, widow.
>
> *Widow.* Without the dangerous help of a parson, I do not fear it, sir.

The whole play, even to the romantic scenes, is just a youngster's game. It is tentative, full of action and boisterousness, alive with gaiety indeed, but the method is not perfected.

In *She Would if She Could* Etherege was much more certain of what he wanted to do. He had begun to see what elements to reject, and in consequence devoted a great deal of space to that delightful quartette, Ariana and Gatty, Courtal and Freeman. The passages where these are involved read like directions for a ballet; it is all a dance; the couples bow, set to partners, perform their evolutions, and bow again; and indeed their value consists in their ability to create this sort of atmosphere. Here is the first meeting of the principal dancers:

> *Court.* Fie, fie! put off these scandals to all good faces.
>
> *Gatty.* For your reputation's sake we shall keep 'em on. 'Slife, we should be taken for your relations if we durst show our faces with you thus publicly.
>
> *Ariana.* And what a shame that would be to a couple of young gallants. Methinks, you should blush to think on't.
>
> *Court.* These were pretty toys, invented, first, merely for the good of us poor lovers to deceive the jealous, and to blind the malicious; but the proper use is so wickedly perverted, that it makes all honest men hate the fashion mortally.
>
> *Free.* A good face is as seldom covered with a vizard-mask, as a good hat with an oiled case. And yet, on my conscience, you are both handsome.

> *Court.* Do but remove 'em a little, to satisfy a foolish scruple.
>
> *Ariana.* This is a just punishment you have brought upon yourselves by that unpardonable sin of talking.
>
> *Gatty.* You can only brag now of your acquaintance with a Farendon gown and a piece of black velvet.
>
> *Court.* The truth is, there are some vain fellows whose loose behaviour of late has given great discouragement to the honourable proceedings of all virtuous ladies.
>
> *Free.* But I hope you have more charity than to believe us of the number of the wicked.

And here is another figure:

> *Gatty.* I suppose your mistress, Mr. Courtal, is always the last woman you are acquainted with.
>
> *Court.* Do not think, madam, I have that false measure of my acquaintance which poets have of their verses, always to think the last best—though I esteem you so in justice to your merit.
>
> *Gatty.* Or if you do not love her best, you always love to talk of her most ; as a barren coxcomb that wants discourse is ever entertaining company out of the last book he read in.
>
> *Court.* Now you accuse me most unjustly, madam ; who the devil that has common sense will go birding with a clack in his cap.?
>
> *Ariana.* Nay, we do not blame you, gentlemen ; every one in their way ; a huntsman talks of his dogs, a falconer of his hawks, a jockey of his horse, and a gallant of his mistress.
>
> *Gatty.* Without the allowance of this vanity, an amour would soon grow as dull as matrimony.

The very words foot it briskly, taking their ease among horsemen's terms. When Courtal and Freeman first sight Ariana and Gatty in the Mulberry Garden, Freeman says, ' 'Sdeath, how fleet they are ! Whatsoever faults they have they cannot be broken-winded.' And Courtal takes it up, 'Sure, by that little mincing step they should be country fillies that have been breathed a course at park and barley-break.* We shall never reach 'em.' Sir Joslin Jolley, the young ladies' kinsman, describes Gatty as ' a clean-limbed wench,

* A game not unlike Prisoner's Base.

and has neither spavin, splinter nor wind-gall', while Sir Joslin himself is straight from the kennels, and evidently hunts his own hounds. 'Here they are, boys, i' faith', is his method of introducing 'that couple of sly skittish fillies', his wards, to the young gallants, 'heuk! Sly girls and madcap, to 'em, to 'em boys, alou!'

Though full of charm and vivacity, the play was not a success when first acted. Pepys wrote that he heard 'Etheredge, the poet . . . mightily find fault with the actors, that they were out of humour, and had not their parts perfect, and that Harris (who played Sir Joslin) did do nothing', and Shadwell supports the view that it was badly acted. But, indeed, it was difficult for the actors to be *in* humour, for Etherege had fallen between two stools. He had not quite fused the elements of art and life, for side by side with Ariana's fragile world we have the full-blooded boisterousness of Sir Joslin Jolley and Sir Oliver Cockwood. With those boon companions the play could hardly fail to partake of rough and tumble. They are bold, desperate old fellows among women and wine, and Sir Joslin is ever bursting into song which for frankness would not have disgraced our armies in Flanders. The two atmospheres are mutually destructive. Etherege had not yet broken away from the late Elizabethan tradition.

The Cockwoods and Sir Joslin are, for the matter of that, would-be Jonsonian, but they have all the grittiness of Jonsonian characters without their depth. What are we to make of this scene, where Lady Cockwood is in company with the young ladies and their gallants, Sir Joslin, and Sentry, her 'gentlewoman'?

> *Sir Oliver (strutting).* Dan, dan, da, ra, dan, &c. Avoid my presence! the very sight of that face makes me more impotent than an eunuch.

Lady Cock. Dear Sir Oliver (*offering to embrace him*).

Sir Oliver. Forbear your conjugal clippings; I will have a wench; thou shalt fetch me a wench, Sentry.

Sentry. Can you be so inhuman to my dear lady?

Sir Oliver. Peace, Envy, or I will have thee executed for petty treason; thy skin flayed off, stuffed and hung up in my hall in the country, as a terror to my whole family.

It is no wonder that after the scene in the Mulberry Garden the actors were a little puzzled; it is too brutal, and the punishment that follows upon Sir Oliver's misdemeanour is humorous fantasy, certainly, but a little crude in idea. His clothes are locked up, with the exception of his 'penitential suit', an old-fashioned, worn-out garment in which he dare not stir abroad.

Lady Cockwood, who gives the play its title, is an unpleasant character, not clearly conceived. The 'noble laziness of the mind', of which Etherege was so proud, forbade him to deal ably with things he did not like. Since he was no satirist (until he went to Ratisbon), and did not feel impelled to criticize manners—which after all suited him admirably—he could only touch well what he could touch lovingly. And he did not love Lady Cockwood. She was a woman eager for amorous adventure, and equally eager to preserve her 'honour'; so far good. But Courtal, whom she pursued ferociously, found her 'the very spirit of impertinence, so foolishly fond and troublesome, that no man above sixteen is able to endure her'. Alas! the poor soul had not got the technique of the Restoration game; she could not pretend to deny.

On the other hand, there is plenty of fun to be got out of her, and Courtal's evasions of her addresses are full of ingenuity. The figure of the man who, as his name implies, was not over selective, pursued by a woman he cannot endure, provides a good case of the Meredithan comic.

But the best scene of all, where she is concerned, takes place in an eating-house. She has gone there with Courtal, Freeman, and the two young ladies, leaving Sir Oliver safe at home in his penitential suit. But though he had ' intended to retire into the pantry and there civilly to divert himself at backgammon with the butler', Sir Joslin lures him forth with the promise of good wine, and women not so good, to the very place where Lady Cockwood has gone. Her ladyship outmanœuvres her husband, and bursts upon him with all the colours of offended virtue flying bravely. After a counterfeited swoon she breaks out :

> Perfidious man ; I am too tame and foolish. Were I every day at the plays, the Park and Mulberry Garden, with a kind look secretly to indulge the unlawful passion of some young gallant ; or did I associate myself with the gaming madams, and were every afternoon at my Lady Brief's and my Lady Meanwell's at ombre and quebas, pretending ill-luck to borrow money of a friend, and then pretending good luck to excuse the plenty to a husband, my suspicious demeanour had deserved this ; but I who out of a scrupulous tenderness to my honour, and to comply with thy base jealousy, have denied myself all those blameless recreations which a virtuous lady might enjoy, to be thus inhumanly reviled in my own person, and thus unreasonably robbed and abused in thine too !

Such admirable prose from a lady so little able to manage her affairs astonishes Courtal. ' Sure she will take up anon, or crack her mind, or else the devil's in it ', he remarks. And here we see the value of the restraint Etherege had learned ; the Elizabethan scene might have romped away with him to the regions of farce, but seeing the danger he pulled it together with some neat phrasing. The *jeunes premiers* and their partners are calming Lady Cockwood after her outburst against her husband :

> *Aria.* How bitterly he weeps ! how sadly he sighs !
> *Gatty.* I daresay he counterfeited his sin, and is real in his repentance.

Court. Compose yourself a little, pray Madam; all this was mere raillery, a way of talk, which Sir Oliver, being well bred, has learned among the gay people of the town.

Free. If you did but know, Madam, what an odious thing it is to be thought to love a wife in good company, you would easily forgive him.

What charming wit! and how naïvely Etherege seems to believe in the argument himself!

The above may show how Etherege laughed with delight at the entertaining thing life was. Neither it nor his plays were to be taken too seriously. Both were vastly amusing things, and sex comedy like the frolicking of lambs. He rarely makes an appeal to the intellect. Yet there are two or three notes in this play that, wittingly or not, cause that deeper laughter, provoked by man's realization of his own helplessness against his desires, the laughter at the triumph of man's body over his mind Schlegel found at the root of all comedy. Thus when the young ladies are finally engaged, Sir Joslin asks, ' Is it a match, boys ? ' and Courtal replies, ' if the heart of man be not very deceitful, 'tis very likely it may be so '.

After this play Etherege was silent for eight years, and in the interval two things had happened ; he had become less boisterous, his pleasures were becoming those of the intellect rather than those of the healthy animal seeking ' wild pleasures ' as an outlet for his energies; and at the same time he had begun to weary a little of the game, so that here and there we have a display of sheer bad temper. He was no longer so young as he had been, and perhaps the life led by ' gentle George ' was beginning to tell on his nerves. But if in his weariness he would have liked solitude, he could not endure dullness. If it can be said he was afflicted by any sort of *Weltschmerz*, he knew of no method to dissipate it other than a brawl, such as the one which, in the year *The Man of Mode* appeared, culminated in the death of one of the participators. So, as already in the rough and tumble of his earlier comedies we find a spice of brutality underlying the laughter, in his last play there is now and again a harshness that is in danger of spoiling it. When he writes such a sentence as ' I have of late lived as chaste as my Lady Etherege ', we get a hint of the state of mind that produced the Dorimant-Mrs. Loveit scenes in *The Man of Mode*. We may take the first, where Dorimant, determined to break relations with his mistress for the sake of her ' friend ' Belinda, sets to work :

Loveit. Faithless, inhuman, barbarous man !
Dor. Good, now, the alarm strikes—
Loveit. Without sense of love, of honour, or of gratitude, tell me—for I will know—what devil, masked she, were you with at the play yesterday ?
Dor. Faith, I resolved as much as you, but the devil was obstinate and would not tell me.
Loveit. False in this as in your vows to me ! You do know.
Dor. The truth is, I did all I could to know.
Loveit. And dare you own it to my face ? Hell and furies— (*tears her fan in pieces*)
Dor. Spare your fan, madam ; you are growing hot, and will want it to cool you.
Loveit. Horror and distraction seize you, sorrow and remorse gnaw your soul, and punish all your perjuries to me (*Weeps*).
Dor. So thunder breaks the clouds in twain
    And makes a passage for the rain.

This is no longer in comedy vein ; it is too cruel. It was no wonder that Belinda, herself the ' devil, masked she ', declared :

He 's given me the proof I desired of his love :
    But 'tis a proof of his ill-nature too ;
    I wish I had not seen him use her so.

But the ill-nature does not stop there, and Dorimant becomes an outrageous bully. He gets Belinda to induce

Loveit to walk in the Mall that he may cause her to make
a fool of herself with Sir Fopling. Even Belinda protests,
' You persecute her too much ', but the excuse is that ' You
women make 'em (the afflictions in love), who are commonly as unreasonable in that as you are at play; without
the advantage be on your side, a man can never quietly
give over when he is weary '. This is sex-antagonism with
a vengeance; we are down to bedrock here, and thus
expressed it is not very laughable. There is too much spite
in it.

At the same time Mrs. Loveit is an amazingly natural
presentation of a jealous woman, struggling fiercely against
her fate. She did not deserve to be told in public by
Harriet, her successful rival, a charming coquette full of
womanly wisdom, that ' Mr. Dorimant has been your God
Almighty long enough ', and that she must find another
lover, or, better still, betake herself to a nunnery! Yet this
only harshness in an otherwise admirable comedy may not
have appeared a flaw to the audiences of those days. Those
scenes may have induced the laughter of common sense
which the writer of comedy can rarely escape, but for us
they spoil the delight. After all, Etherege could do better
on the theme:

> It is not, Celia, in our power
> To say how long our love will last;
> It may be we within this hour
> May lose those joys we now do taste;
> The blessed, that immortal be,
> From change in love are only free.
>
> Then since we lovers mortal are,
> Ask not how long our love will last;
> But while it does let us take care
> Each minute be with pleasure pass'd:
> Were it not madness to deny
> To live, because we're sure to die?

the perfect expression of Etherege's philosophy of love—
and life. For even in this comedy he could keep the sentiment on the lyric level, as when Emilia says, ' Do not vow
—Our love is frail as is our life and full as little in our power ;
and are you sure you shall outlive this day ? '

To turn to Dorimant. He is a marvellous erotic, with
' more mistresses now depending than the most eminent
lawyer in England has causes '. ' Constancy at my years ! '
he cries. ' You might as well expect the fruit the autumn
ripens in the spring.' He has, moreover, the courage of
his philosophy. ' When love grows diseased the best thing
we can do is to put it to a violent death ; I cannot endure
the torture of a lingering and consumptive passion.' He is
master of all the technique of feminine conquest ; he can
pique as well as caress and insinuate, and his method of
attack on Harriet is blunt. Loving her to the distraction of
marriage—though even here he must excuse himself on the
plea that it will ' repair the ruins of my estate '—he attempts the satiric. He tells her :

> I observed how you were pleased when the fops cried, She's
> handsome, very handsome, by God she is, . . . then to make
> yourself more agreeable, how wantonly you played with your
> head, flung back your locks, and look'd smilingly over your
> shoulder at 'em.

Temerarious man, she was more than a match for him, and
retorted with an admirable little sketch of what we cannot
but think an odious gallant :

> I do not go begging the men's, as you do the ladies' good
> liking, with a sly softness in your looks and a gentle slowness
> in your bows as you pass by 'em—as thus, sir—(*acts him*).

For Etherege was a master of witty description : the fat
orange-woman is an ' overgrown jade with a flasket of guts
before her ', or an ' insignificant brandy-bottle ' ; Medley,
as Amelia tells him, is ' a living libel, a breathing lampoon ',

and he is at times ' rhetorically drunk '. This is the bright
current coin of lively description, but Etherege, with his
vivid imagination, can give us wonderful set pieces of
brilliant mimicry. Long before we see Sir Fopling Flutter,
we know exactly what he looks like :

> He was yesterday at the play, with a pair of gloves up to
> his elbow and a periwig more exactly curled than a lady's head
> newly dressed for a ball. . . . His head stands for the most part
> on one side, and his looks are more languishing than a lady's
> when she lolls at stretch in her coach, or leans her head care-
> lessly against the side of a box in the playhouse.

He delighted to observe every pose and gesture, each
revealing intonation. Here, for instance, are Young Bellair
and Harriet instructing one another how to appear charmed
by each other's company, so as to deceive their parents
about their real sentiments. First Bellair has his lesson
from Harriet :

> *Har.* Your head a little more on one side, ease yourself on
> your left leg, and play with your right hand.
> *Bel.* Thus, is it not ?
> *Har.* Now set your right leg firm on the ground, adjust your
> belt, then look about you . . . Smile, and turn to me again very
> sparkish.

Then it is her turn to be instructed :

> *Bel.* Now spread your fan, look down upon it, and tell the
> sticks with a finger . . .
> *Har.* 'Twill not be amiss now to seem a little pleasant.
> *Bel.* Clap your fan then in both your hands, snatch it to
> your mouth, smile, and with a lively motion fling your body a
> little forwards. So—now spread it ; fall back on the sudden, . . .
> take up ! look grave and fall a-fanning of yourself—admirably
> well acted.

Could anything be written with a surer touch, a greater
descriptive acumen ?

Occasionally he touches farce in a manner we must admit
is Molièresque :

Medley. Where does she live?

Orange-W. They lodge at my house.

Medley. Nay, then she's in a hopeful way.

Orange-W. Good Mr. Medley, say your pleasure of me, but take heed how you affront my house. God's my life, in a hopeful way!

Finally, the character of his observation may be seen in Dorimant's remark:

I have known many women make a difficulty of losing a maidenhead, who have afterwards made none of a cuckold.

Or in this letter from Molly:

I have no money, and am very mallicolly, pray send me a guynie to see the operies.

This is life, and its placing makes it art.

The ostensible hero of the play, Sir Fopling Flutter, has little to do with the action. He is the most delicately and sympathetically drawn of all the fops in the great series of coxcombs. He is in himself a delight, presented from pure joy of him, and is not set up merely as a target for the raillery of wiser fools. Unlike Vanbrugh's Lord Foppington, he has no intellectual idea behind his appearance. He exists by his garments and his *calèche*; there is, as it were, no noumenal Flutter. We have his picture:

Lady Town. His gloves are well fringed, large and graceful.

Sir Fop. I was always eminent for being *bien ganté*.

Emilia. He wears nothing but what are originals of the most famous hands in Paris. . . .

Lady Town. The suit?

Sir Fop. Barroy.

Emilia. The garniture?

Sir Fop. Le Gras.

Medley. The shoes?

Sir Fop. Piccat.

Dorimant. The periwig?

Sir Fop. Chedreux.

Lady T. Em. The gloves?

Sir Fop. Orangerie. You know the smell, ladies.

Moreover, all the people around him enjoy him as much as
Etherege himself so evidently did. Life would be the duller
without him, and so his existence is justified. He must
even be encouraged:

> *Sir Fop.* An intrigue now would be but a temptation to throw
> away that vigour on one, which I mean shall shortly make my
> court to the whole sex in a ballet.
> *Medley.* Wisely considered, Sir Fopling.
> *Sir Fop.* No one woman is worth the loss of a cut in a caper.
> *Medley.* Not when 'tis so universally designed.

It is exquisite. Etherege never oversteps the bounds. Sir
Fopling is not for a moment the fatuous ass Vanbrugh's
Lord Foppington becomes. Should he say, ' I cannot passi-
tively tell whether ever I shall speak again or nat', our
attitude would at once become critical. But this one cannot
be with Sir Fopling, who so obviously enjoys himself without any affectation whatever. He is not like Sir Courtly
Nice in Crowne's comedy, who when challenged declared,
' It goes against my stomach horribly to fight such a beast.
Should his filthy sword but touch me, 'twould make me as
sick as a dog.' Etherege was too good an artist for that
kind of exaggeration. He presented, and avoided awakening the critical spirit. Sir Fopling was to him what a rare
orchid is to an enthusiastic gardener, a precious specimen,
and the finger of satire must not be allowed to touch him.
We should be fools to take the trouble to think Sir Fopling
a fool, and to weary of him would be to show ourselves ' a
little too delicate ', like Emilia. It is not as an universal
abstract that he exists, but as a fantasy. To him, and
perhaps to him only, Charles Lamb's remarks are applicable.
No disharmonies of flesh and blood disturb this delicate
creation: no blast of reality dispels the perfumery, or
ruffles the least hair on the inimitable perruque. No
acrimony guided the pen that described him, no word of

common sense reduced him to a right proportion among 'les gens graves et sérieux, les vieillards, et les amateurs de vertu'. To attempt to deduce a lesson from him is as fruitful as to seek a symbol in a primrose, a meaning in the contours of a cloud.

But Etherege was writing comedy, and he could not quite escape the presentment of the happy mean, or an indication of the most comfortable way to live. Bellair, ' always complaisant and seldom impertinent', is to be our model; but even he errs on the side of sentiment, and does not escape the comic censor :

> *Bel.* I could find in my heart to resolve not to marry at all.
> *Dor.* Fie, fie ! that would spoil a good jest, and disappoint the well natured town of an occasion of laughing at you.

Indeed, Etherege, from the ' free ' comedy point of view, was slightly tarnished by experience. 'When your love's grown strong enough to make you bear being laughed at, I'll give you leave to trouble me with it', Harriet tells Dorimant. She was in the right of it there, but it has a serious note, and Medley is ever and anon a little tiresome. To him Sir Fopling is 'a fine-mettled coxcomb, brisk and insipid, pert and dull', but one would weary of Medley sooner than of Sir Fopling. These, however, are only occasional lapses, and even the most sententious remarks are relieved in a spirit of tomfoolery, or lightened with a happier wisdom. When Harriet says ' beauty runs as great a risk exposed at Court as wit does on the stage ', she would have pleased Collier, until she added, ' where the ugly and the foolish all are free to censure', and the sound truths enunciated by Loveit and Dorimant are only by way of weapons against each other. They would be the last to live by their own precepts.

For some reason Etherege has been much neglected. Leigh Hunt did not include him in his famous edition—it was thus his none too blameless life escaped the misrepresentations of Macaulay—nor does he grace the Mermaid collection. But Mr. Gosse and Mr. Palmer have done much to remedy this, and the former has done him full justice as a delicate painter who loved subtle contrasts in ' rose-colour and pale grey ', who delighted in grace and movement and agreeable groupings. It is a frivolous world, Strephon bending on one knee to Chloe, who fans the pink blush on her painted cheek, while Momus peeps with a grimace through the curtains behind her. They form an engaging trio, ' mais ce n'est pas la vie humaine '. Well it is not *la vie humaine* to us nowadays, but if it was such to Dennis (' I allow it to be nature '), how much more so must it have been to the Sedleys, the Rochesters, and the Beau Hewitts! Even Langbaine stated it to be ' as well drawn to the life as any play that has been acted since the restoration of the English stage '. And if Steele said that ' this whole celebrated piece is a perfect contradiction of good manners, good sense, and common honesty ', we must remember that such a play could never appeal to the ' good sense ' of the confectioner of the sentimental comedy.

Etherege, if you will, is a minor writer, in his exuberance nearer Mrs. Behn than to Congreve with his depth. But from another point of view he is far above all the other playwrights of his period, for he did something very rare in our literature. He presented life treated purely as an appearance: there was no more meaning in it apart from its immediate reactions than there is in a children's game of dumb-crambo. This sort of comedy, while it is realistic in semblance, and faithfully copies the outward aspects of the time, creates an illusion of life that is far removed from reality. Here is no sense of grappling with circumstance, for man is unencumbered by thoughts or passions. Life is a merry-go-round, and there is no need to examine the machinery or ponder on the design. It is not play for the sake of exercise, but play for its own sake, and the game must not be allowed to become too arduous. Nor is it life seen at a distance, but the forms of those known and liked seen intimately from a shady arbour in an old, sunny garden. Butterflies hover against the wall, and the sound of the *viol da gamba* floats serenely over the scent-laden atmosphere, while the figures, absorbed in their own youth, bend gracefully to the movements of the bourrée or sarabande. *Eheu fugaces!* Yes, now and again: but the idle thought passes in the ripples of laughter, and the solemn motto on the sundial is hidden beneath the roses.

VI

WYCHERLEY

Born 1640.
Love in a Wood, 1671 (written 1659?).
The Gentleman Dancing Master, 1672 (written 1662?).
The Country Wife, 1675.
The Plain Dealer, 1676 (written 1666? and 1676).
Died 1716.

PERHAPS no figure in the Restoration period appears so
strange as that of Wycherley. What are we to make of
the character of this handsome person, endowed, as Pope
said, with so much of the ' nobleman look ', yet a being all
angles and unwieldy muscular lumps, shot with unexpected
streaks of grace? Certainly he had something of the giant
deformity of Chapman, his great love of physical life, with
its thew and bone and warm rushing blood, but all tinged
with a deep pessimism, a fierce hatred, the *saeva indignatio*
of Swift. He was for ever striving after the absolute, but
always bewildered as to which extreme to choose. Born a
Protestant, he became a Catholic in his early youth in
France, and on his return became Protestant once more.
Perhaps he went to sea and fought against the Dutch, but
at any rate, we see him at the age of thirty-two carried to
Court by the Duchess of Cleveland, the irresistible Castle-
maine, where, probably not quite at his ease, yet wondering
if life lived like that might not after all be the best, he
seems to us like some splendid uncut diamond amid the
polished stones. Outwardly he is the outspoken witty man
of fashion, admirably suited to shine in a brilliant court ;

yet all the while he is producing plays wherein uncouth figures rush upon the stage reviling one another as though engaged in some hopeless, desperate effort to be something absolute, whatever it may be; monsters held up to ridicule, yet which somehow have a quality that makes the laugher ridiculous. Court advancement, then, suddenly, semi-clandestine marriage with the Countess of Drogheda, who kept him a sort of prisoner, allowing him to go to the tavern opposite only on condition that the windows should be open that she might see what company he kept—and silence. Literary obscurity, with a vast reputation echoing portentously through the galleries of Whitehall, and, after his wife's death, for some years disappearance from society in a debtor's prison, whence he was relieved by the king. Then, in late life, he is found standing in front of his picture by Lely and murmuring *Quantum mutatus ab illo*, and making Montaigne, La Rochefoucauld, and Seneca his daily reading. Though impulsively generous and firm in friendship, once Dryden has gone there is no intimate left. We see him presiding at Will's, but he has outlived his time, and the young men pay homage to the ghost of Plautus and Terence embodied in an infirm figure who would not be painted without his periwig. Then, hopelessly debilitated in memory, we find him asking a ' little, tender, and crazy carcass' endowed with genius, Pope, to help him with his verses, getting furiously angry at his corrections, then apologizing, almost in adoration. Finally, a death-bed marriage with a young woman, so that he may pay his debts, set up a youthful couple whom he liked, and in so doing ' plague his damned nephew' with encumbered estates. And on this death-bed he received extreme unction from a Catholic priest, and made his young bride swear never again to marry an old man.

He wrote his first two plays when very young, and a third at the age of twenty-five, but he kept them by him until he was thirty-one. Up to that time, after his return from France where he had come into touch with the best cultured society, he seems to have led a life of retirement at the University and elsewhere. This satisfied one side of his nature, the brooding side that saw the value of the puritanic outlook, but not the other side, that dominated by his healthy, desiring body. He was allured by the fashionable aspect of London life, with its strange excitements and voluptuous excesses. If he had a play acted he would certainly be involved in this society—and where would it lead? Plays were dangerous things, and did he even like them? He could never be sure of his values, and could not for a long time make up his mind to take the plunge, for he knew there were no half-measures for him. The nothing or the all! But at last, no longer able to resist the impulse, he dared, and polishing up his two early plays—he was not quite satisfied with the third, it was weightier—he brought them up to date and went on, outwardly bold.

His first three plays, counting *The Plain Dealer* as his third, reveal all his strange revulsions against the society in which he now lived as fully as any. Did he repent having ventured into this lurid light? For this John Fox masquerading in the habiliments of a Charles Sedley—or should it be the other way round?—seems very strange. He is like a Dante strayed into the gardens of Boccaccio, but unable to forget for a moment the plague raging everywhere. Which of the two tugging impulses was it better to obey? On which side was he to use his vigorous intellect? It is this gnawing doubt which makes it so difficult to see what he meant by his plays, what he was trying to do. A learner in the Spanish school, unrivalled in the management of plot (here Congreve at his best is a bungler to him), he was master of the unities of time and place, but in the essential unity, that of atmosphere, he failed. Indeed, his plays, with the exception of *The Country Wife*, are the strangest hotch-potch. At one moment we are interested in the development of the story, then we are treated to an exhibition of virulent satire, now beguiled with the antics of a superbly ludicrous fop, entertained with the fencing of a coquettish tongue, or plunged into a bath of tepid romance.

It is his satire that is most interesting, and in it he differs from others who write in that vein, for his satire is never that of a prig, and it is characteristic of him that he always seems to include himself in his denunciations. Some of his writing reads suspiciously like self-flagellation, or even *nostalgie de la boue*, as though he needed to expiate. Involved in the manners of a society he now hated, now loved, he could not forbear reviling even himself. He scourged his sensuality with a brutal whip, and like a scorpion surrounded by a ring of fire, turned his sting upon himself.

His first play need not detain us long. It is obviously the work of a brilliant young man, and is not unlike a Shirley play in manner and idea, though it is much more virile. However, the intricacy of its plot, the rather clumsy handling of the humours, as in Sir Simon Addlepot or Lady Flippant, and the at times boorish repartee, make it on the whole tedious reading, though it might act more briskly. The scabrous passages seem badly aimed, as though Wycherley himself did not quite know with what object they were there. Macaulay said he attempted to make vice pleasant, but on reading this we can only think that Macaulay must have had a queer taste in vice. Its mere exposition, as in the case of Mrs. Crossbite, ' an old cheating jill, and bawd to her daughter', unredeemed by criticism of any kind, can serve neither the purposes of pleasure or those of philosophy. That the play is full of life cannot be denied, but it lacks joyousness. Wycherley was not a poet in the sense of one who seeks for beauty, and in this play, although he did not yet hate his characters, he treated them with a cold disdain. Evelyn wrote later:

> As long as men are false and women vain,
> While gold continues to be virtue's bane,
> In pointed satire Wycherley shall reign.

But, in truth, Wycherley's weapon was rounded at the point; he used, not a rapier, but a bludgeon. Vitality he had abundantly, but when he wrote this play grace was sadly lacking in him.

Already in this early play we get passages of that bitter satire he was afterwards to wield furiously ; but in direct contrast we may get such a delightful scene as that where Dapperwit hunting for a simile is treated in the lightest manner of critical comedy. Mrs. Martha, to whom he is secretly paying his addresses is in an agony of apprehension lest her father should come and catch them together. She is imploring him to go :

Dap. Peace ! Peace !

Mar. What are you thinking of ?

Dap. I am thinking what a wit without vanity is like. He is like—

Mar. You do not think we are in a public place, and may be surprised and prevented by my father's scouts.

Dap. What ! would you have me lose my thought ?

Mar. You would rather lose your mistress, it seems.

Dap. He is like—I think I am a sot to-night, let me perish.

Mar. Nay, if you are so in love with your thought—

(Offers to go.)

Dap. Are you so impatient to be my wife ? He is like—he is like—a picture without shadows, or—or—a face without patches

—or a diamond without a foil. These are new thoughts now, these are new!

Mar. You are wedded to your thoughts already, I see; good night.

Dap. Madam, do not take it ill,
> For loss of happy thought there's no amends,
> For his new jest true wit will lose old friends.

That's new again—the thought's new. (*Exeunt.*)

This is admirable in the farcical style; but then side by side with it we have the romantic true-love plot, rather involved, of Christina and Valentine, the latter jealous enough to be 'still turning the dagger's point on himself', a touch in much deeper vein which begins to go to the root of the Restoration dis-ease. It is this story, one guesses, that is meant to make the appeal to common sense, to the happy mean of the classical school. But its introduction is unconvincing, its figures shadowy, and it may be that this was a legacy from later Elizabethan work.

''Tis not sufficient to make the hearer laugh aloud, although there is a certain merit even in this', so Wycherley, quoting Horace, prefaced his next comedy, by now fully aware of a moral purpose. But there is little literary or moral merit in the laughter aroused by *The Gentleman Dancing Master*, for we laugh for the most part only at the farcical elements of the intrigue, and this soon becomes wearisome. In this adaptation from the Spanish, Wycherley had his technique perfected; there is only one slight flaw in a complicated structure. But no wit is needed to see his points; they are too laboured. We may take a small instance of his Frenchified fop, Monsieur de Paris, an Englishman who had spent a few months in the French capital. He enters:

Monsieur. Serviteur! Serviteur! la cousine; I come to give the *bon soir*, as the French say.

Hippolita. O, cousin, you know him; the fine gentleman they talk so much of in town.

> *Monsieur.* I know all the *beau monde*, cousine.
> *Hippolita.* Master—
> *Monsieur.* Monsieur Taileur, Monsieur Esmit, Monsieur . . .
> *Hippolita.* These are Frenchmen.
> *Monsieur.* Non, non ; voud you have me say Mr. Taylor, Mr. Smith ? Fi ! fi ! *tete non.*

It is so overdone that it ceases even to be funny, and the Spanish ' humour ' conflicting with the French ' humour ' is mere verbal knock-about, although this constitutes one of the chief ideas of the play :

> *Don Diego.* While you wear pantaloons, you are beneath my passion, *voto*—auh—they make thee look and waddle (with all those geegaw ribbons) like a great, old, fat, slovenly water-dog.
> *Monsieur.* And your Spanish hose, and your nose in the air, make you look like a great, grizzled, long Irish greyhound reaching a crust from off a high shelf, ha ! ha ! ha !

This is not the language of formal fops, such as these men are supposed to be, but rather that of farmers in a tavern brawl ; perhaps this was purposely done, but for all its excellent vigour, it is fatal to the comic atmosphere of which we occasionally get a puff in other parts of the play. Don Diego Formal, however, is fairly consistent with himself, and though clumsy, is more than any other of Wycherley's characters in the right tradition of Jonson. The final scene, where rather than have it thought he had been gulled, or that anybody could possibly know better than he, he gives away half his fortune as a dowry, is really a stroke of original genius :

> And that you may see I deceived you all along, and you not me, ay, and am able to deceive you still, for I know how you think I will give you little or nothing with my daughter, like other fathers, since you have married without my consent—but I say, I'll deceive you now ; for you shall have the most part of my estate in present, and the rest at my death.—There 's for you : I think I have deceived you now, look you.

As one reads this play one cannot help wishing that he had held fast to the ' certain merit ', and had let whatever he might, in his youth, have thought profound take care of itself. For he can make us laugh delightedly at the absurd exaggeration of an idea. Besides the farcical side, and the fun we get from our human delight in intrigue, there are touches of the highest critical comedy in which we get something much more than a vision of the dull, obstinate, gullible nature of man. Here is the Mrs. Caution—Hippolita scene in the first act.

Hip. I never lived so wicked a life as I have done this twelve-month since I have not seen a man. [*She is aged fourteen !*]

Mrs. C. How, how ! if you have not seen a man, how could you be wicked ? How could you do any ill ?

Hip. No, I have done no ill ; but I have paid it with thinking . . . But know, I have those thoughts sleeping and waking ; for I have dreamt of a man.

Mrs. C. No matter, no matter—so that it was but a dream....

Hip. But I did not only dream—(*Sighs.*)

Mrs. C. How, how ! . . . confess. . . .

Hip. Well, I will then. Indeed, aunt, I did not only dream, but I was pleased with my dream . . . to be delighted when we wake with a naughty dream, is a sin, aunt ; and I am so very scrupulous, that I would as soon consent to a naughty man as to a naughty dream.

Thought dances here, moved by springs of insight—and in those days Freud was not ; but underlying all there is a hatred Wycherley has for Hippolita because she has the desires natural to the animal. He still could not make up his mind which world to choose. To Etherege life was a thing one took as it came, and made as amusing as possible ; and if one was in the end a little disillusioned, one sought refreshment in the graceful and fantastic. But Wycherley's joy was spoiled by his puritanism, and this in turn was cankered by scepticism. Both joy and puritanism were bogeys to him; he hated the man of fashion as much as he did the fanatic, and if he preached the happy mean, as he did in this play through the victorious Englishman, it was not from the gently serious conviction of Molière, nor from an intellectual adoption as with Shadwell, but because on either side lay a trap too hideous to contemplate. In this play he laughed, it is true, yet one feels that if he had not, he would have, not wept, but raged. What strange dialogues, for instance, take place between Don Diego and his sister :

> *Don D.* Nay, with your favour, mistress, I'll ask him now.
> *Mrs. C.* Y'facks, but you shan't. I'll ask him, and ask you no favour, that I will.
> *Don D.* Y'fackins, but you shan't ask him! if you go there too, look you, you prattle box, you, I'll ask him.
> *Mrs. C.* I will ask him, I say.

It is like the personages of *Gammer Gurton's Needle*, curiously clothed, intruding their humours upon the subtler distinctions of the cultivated man, producing an atmosphere curiously at variance with that of sophisticated *double entendre*.

The truth is that in these two plays Wycherley could not bear his fools; they irritated him beyond measure, and in a manner that debarred him from any sympathetic understanding of them. There was an icy deliberateness about him, an appalling consistency in his view of the characters, and it is through this that he becomes, if not a poet, at least a creator. He belongs to the prig-comedy school, but he has no personal arrogance. His satire almost reaches the level of fanaticism. It was not enough to make the spectators laugh; the poor, doubting beast felt impelled to make them brood upon their vices also. Or did he think that by steeping himself in the mud he would achieve some kind of catharsis ?

The applause which greeted Wycherley's first play (for

the second proved a failure) induced him to write another,
The Country Wife, and this play he gave to be acted next.
It is his mature piece, the final thing he had to say; and
thus when he was asked for a fourth, all he could do was to
rewrite his third, *The Plain Dealer*, introducing as he did
so a ' critique of *The Country Wife* '. Since this is the earlier
play we will take it next.

The Plain Dealer is certainly founded on *Le Misanthrope*,
but Wycherley re-thought it all, and made it into something
quite different. Yet his choice must surely have been due
to something in Molière's play that appealed irresistibly to
him. Alceste, out of touch with the society in which he
moved, how much he was Wycherley himself! Alceste who
craved honesty above all things, was not this also Wycherley with his reputation for outspokenness ? But *The Plain
Dealer* is much more than a mere copy. For Wycherley
threw himself into the character, and with his rage for the
absolute came to an extreme of furious passion, imagining
himself in the worst conceivable situations, so that every
event would prove him right in his indignation. But this
was not enough. Manly himself, with none of the hope
that buoyed up Alceste to the last, incapable of that final
touching appeal to Olivia that Alceste made to Célimène
(though, indeed, the situation of Olivia made such a thing
impossible), must be made to appear as loathsome as the
rest, as untrustworthy, and much more brutal. There is no
happy mean; there is no Philinte—for Freeman is an
unscrupulous cozener—while Eliza, the Éliante of *Le
Misanthrope*, is scarcely more than a lay figure. But on the
other hand there is Fidelia, that curious evocation from
Fletcherian romance, in which again Wycherley strove after
some absolute. She is a delicate, hardly real figure, obviously
not believed in as are the others, flitting through the play

as an angel might flit through purgatory if conjured up in
the imagination of a tortured soul.

This play is a strange, thorny monster, tearing the flesh
of life wherever it touches it, as it were deliberately, to
reveal the skeleton; an ungainly monster, sprawling all
over society. Now it consists of an act in the Law Courts,
an act only accidentally connected with the play; now of
the grim scenes of Olivia's rape and Vernish's duplicity;
now of the Widow Blackacre, a 'humour' if ever there was
one; now of passages that are pure comedy of manners.
And finally there is Fidelia masquerading as a man so as to
follow the man she loves. How is criticism to approach
this play?

Let us first compare Manly with Alceste; the former,
as Voltaire said, drawn with bolder and less delicate strokes
than the latter. There is no real desire in Manly for a better
state of things, but rather a kind of savage delight in find-
ing things as bad as they are. He is, in the words of Leigh
Hunt, ' a ferocious sensualist who believed himself as great
a rascal as he thought everybody else'. Manly would never
be polite to a bad sonneteer, you never hear him hedging
to avoid telling an unpleasant truth, as Alceste does in the
'Je ne dis pas cela' scene, for Manly would ' rather do a
cruel thing than an unjust one'. It is not that he is too
delicate for the society in which he moves, it is that he is
not subtle enough. Take, for instance, the reactions of the
two men to betrayed love. This is Alceste's despair after
seeing Célimène's letter to Oronte:

> Ah, tout est ruiné ;
> Je suis, je suis trahi, je suis assassiné !
> Célimène . . eût-on pu croire cette nouvelle ?
> Célimène me trompe, et n'est qu'une infidèle.

This is Manly, after Fidelia reports Olivia has kissed ' him ':

Damned, damned woman, that could be so false and infamous! And damned, damned heart of mine, that cannot yet be false, though so infamous! . . . Her love!—a whore's, a witch's love!—but what, did she not kiss well, sir? I'm sure I thought her lips—but I must not think of 'em more—but yet they are such I could still kiss—grow to—and then tear off with my teeth, grind 'em into mammocks, and spit 'em into her cuckold's face.

Or contrast Célimène with Olivia. Célimène is an arrant flirt but we are drawn to her; she is very human. Olivia, on the other hand, is a mere depraved wretch, combining something worse than the lightheartedness of Célimène with the false prudery of Arsinoë. She has promised her hand to Manly, who gives her all his wealth to keep when he goes to sea. But as soon as he has gone she marries his trusted friend Vernish, and between them they steal Manly's money. Within a month of their marriage she tries to cuckold him with Fidelia, and there is a strong presumption that she has already done so with Novel and Plausible. Alceste proposes to revenge himself on Célimène by offering his heart to Éliante. Such a revenge is impossible for Manly, because, since Olivia hates him, it will be no revenge; and so, since she will not admit him to illicit love, he will, by a stratagem, 'lie with her, and call it revenge, for that is honourable', to which performance he will invite his friends, to see her exposed. This is the man Wycherley described in the list of characters as being 'of an honest, surly, nice humour'. His niceties are not apparent, his surliness is unredeemed savagery.

All through the play men are stripped naked, to reveal, not the human animal, but the inhuman brute: the virulence is absolutely ruthless. Not a motive shown, but is to be named rapacity, meanness, fear, lust (except Fidelia's), all hidden or aided by society manners. The law is but an instrument of money-sucking injustice supported by false witnesses; love but physical desire; social intercourse trading in the flesh; and friendship, well, listen to Manly:

> Not but I know that generally no man can be a great enemy but under the name of friend; and if you are a cuckold, it is your friend only that makes you so, for your enemy is not admitted to your house; if you are cheated in your fortune, 'tis your friend that does it, for your enemy is not made your trustee; if your honour or good name be injured, 'tis your friend that does it still, because your enemy is not believed against you.

This is the wild lashing of some tortured creature that cannot understand why it is being hurt. It must be the earlier written part of the play, for later, as in the inter-polated scenes and in *The Country Wife*, Wycherley was reaching at something different. And here and there we get scenes that are in a deliciously light vein. This, for instance, is Lord Plausible's rule for detraction:

> I, like an author in a dedication, never speak well of a man for his sake, but my own; I will not disparage any man, to disparage myself: for to speak ill of people behind their backs, is not like a person of honour; and, truly, to speak ill of 'em to their faces, is not like a complaisant person. But if I did say or do an ill thing to anybody, it should be sure to be behind their backs, out of pure good manners.

He also uses the more familiar method of the comedy of manners, but even this has a vein of acerbity. Here are Olivia, Eliza, and Lettice:

> *Eliz.* But what d'ye think of visits—balls?
> *Oliv.* O, I detest 'em.
> *Eliz.* Of plays?
> *Oliv.* I abominate 'em; filthy, obscene, hideous things.
> *Eliz.* What say you to masquerading in the winter, and Hyde Park in the summer?
> *Oliv.* Insipid pleasures I taste not.
> *Eliz.* Nay, if you are for more solid pleasures, what think you of a rich young husband?

Oliv. O horrid! marriage! what a pleasure you have found out! I nauseate it of all things. [*She has just been secretly married.*]

Let. What does your ladyship think then of a liberal, handsome young lover?

Oliv. A handsome young fellow, you impudent! begone out of my sight. Name a handsome young fellow to me! foh, a hideous handsome young fellow I abominate. [*She is at the time attempting to seduce Fidelia.*]

But these patches of sunlight in a sombre landscape are rare. The more usual effect is such as that produced by the Widow Blackacre, a strange figure eaten up with litigious desires, ready for any imposture that will enable her to win one of her many cases. One is not surprised that her son Jerry is merely a vicious little beast. She is drawn with cold horror that reminds one more of Honoré de Balzac than of Racine. This is how she refuses offers of marriage, refuses, as she puts it, to be put under covert-baron, a state, that is, in which she will not be able to plead her own cases. First she replies to Major Oldfox:

First, I say, for you, major, my walking hospital of an ancient foundation; thou bag of mummy, that wouldst fall asunder, if 'twere not for thy cerecloths . . .

Thou withered, hobbling, distorted cripple; nay, thou art a cripple all over: would'st thou make me the staff of thy age, the crutch of thy decrepidness? me . . .

Thou senseless, impertinent, quibbling, drivelling, feeble, paralytic, impotent, fumbling, frigid nincompoop! . . .

Would'st thou make a caudle-maker, a nurse of me? can't you be bed-rid without a bed-fellow? won't your swan-skins, furs, flannels, and the scorched trencher, keep you warm there? would you have me your Scotch warming-pan, with a pox to you! me—

And then to Freeman:

You would have me keep you, that you might turn keeper; for poor widows are only used like bawds by you: you go to church with us but to get other women to lie with. In fine, you are a cheating, cozening spendthrift, &c.!

Indeed, the greater part of the play is a flow of invective. Wycherley does not preach, he indicts. To what purpose? To redeem mankind? Hardly, for he has here no example of the happy mean, and indicates no line of conduct to increase social convenience. He is not the preserver of social illusions, nor the wielder of the sword of common sense; nor does he create a fairy world in which all that is necessary is to be comely and to talk wittily. He is far from Etherege, he has thrown off Molière. His laughter affords no release, for it is too deeply cynical; it is of the kind that is man's defence against complete disillusion, but it is too twisted to purge of discontent.

'Ridicule,' he prefaced, once more from Horace, 'ridicule commonly decides great matters more forcibly and better than severity'. But what are the great matters, and at what is the ridicule directed? Not at society, at foibles, or vanity, but at mankind itself. And is it ridicule for the more part? Hazlitt surely was right when he said, 'It is a most severe and poignant moral satire . . . a discipline of humanity. . . . It penetrates to the core.' That is how Wycherley would like it felt. And Hazlitt also said that, 'no one can read the play attentively without being the better for it as long as he lives'. But an unrelieved vision of all the mean and sordid aspects of humanity does little to free us from them. We are likely to feel ourselves the more irrevocably imprisoned in despondency. The play reads like a cry of despair. Wycherley was not here among those who can stride across high mountains, and, like Zarathustra, 'laugh at all tragedies whether of the stage or of life'. They hurt him too much.

'The satire, wit, and strength of Manly Wycherley,' Dryden wrote; 'But is railing satire, Novel?' Manly himself asks, 'and roaring and making a noise humour?' No, railing is not satire, for in satire, however low the depths

shown, there is always the intense yearning for something
different, a vision of the immensely moving quality of human
folly, vice, and suffering, as in Swift. But in *The Plain
Dealer* there is none of this : it is a cry not of strength, but
of weakness, the voice of humanity outraged. But Fidelia ?
it will be asked. She is certainly not a pander of the baser
sort, as Macaulay splenetically called her, but a touching
figure :

> Forced to beg that which kills her, if obtained,
> And give away her lover not to lose him.

Yet there is some excuse for Macaulay's error, because the
modicum of absolute good is overwhelmed by the flood of
absolute evil that dominates every act.

When the play was printed, Wycherley dedicated it to
a famous procuress, rising to a piece of splendid irony, for
which he may have taken the hint from a biting passage in
The Dutch Courtezan. And the reason for choosing this person is that

> you, in fine, madam, are no more a hypocrite than I am when
> I praise you ; therefore I doubt not will be thought (even
> by yours and the play's enemies, the nicest ladies) to be the
> fittest patroness for,
>
> Madam,
> Your ladyship's most obedient, faithful, humble servant, and
> THE PLAIN DEALER.

If in his first three plays Wycherley had not yet purged
himself of the elements which interfered with the expression
of his dominating self ; if he had never been sure how he
wanted a scene felt, in *The Country Wife* it is different. In
it he compressed all that his forceful character had shown
him in Restoration society. It is the one play in the whole
period equal to *The Way of the World* in completeness of expression. It is a masterpiece, and here Wycherley did attain
unity of atmosphere. It is a staggering performance, and

never for one instant did he swerve from his point of view.
From beginning to end Wycherley saw clearly what it was
he wanted to do, for now he understood that the real point
of interest in Restoration society was the sex question. He
took scenes from the *École des Femmes* and the *École des
Maris*, but the theme throughout is the failure to rationalize
sex. Horner, the principal figure, takes a leaf out of the
Eunuchus of Terence, and declaring himself impotent, de-
votes himself to living up to his name. From this we get
the whole gallery of Restoration figures—the jealous man
who is proved wrong to be jealous; the trusting man who
is a fool to be so trusting; the light ladies concerned for
their 'honour'; the gay sparks devoted only to their
pleasure; the ignorant woman seduced; the woman of
common sense baffled—the only triumphant figure Horner
himself, the type of all that is most unselectively lecherous,
and who seems to derive such a sorry enjoyment from his
success. We never laugh *at* Horner, just as we never laugh
at Tartufe, though we may on occasion laugh *with* each of
them. Both are grim, nightmare figures, dominating the
helpless, hopeless apes who call themselves civilized men.
Again, the absolute. Again we feel that no mean is possible, because a mean cannot exist for figures which seem
automata animated by devils that drive them irresistibly to
an extreme—and leave them there, to laugh fiendishly. Is
it a comedy at all? Not in the ordinary sense. The clever,
cynical dialogue, the scathing irony, the remorseless strip-
ping of all grace from man, are too overpowering.

Yet on a second reading something else seems to emerge.
For no longer is every word a curse, every phrase an imprecation. Some other quality is there: one is tempted to
say some humanity has crept in. There is, for instance, the
charming figure of Alithea, trying to be honest and reason-

able, the one congenial human being Wycherley ever drew. But the change is not so much in character as in feeling: the sense of torture, of evil one might say, has gone. Wycherley has shouldered the burden that was crushing him. He even tosses it aloft, displaying his huge strength in fantastic wrestlings with the hated thing. A titanic gaiety rushes him along; almost he sees life whole: if he is not reconciled, he is at least no longer personally involved.

But across this acceptance there sometimes cuts a savage snarl. When Horner asks Pinchwife whether, after all, keeping is not better than marriage, the following interchange takes place:

Pin. A pox on't! The jades would jilt me, I could never keep a whore to myself.
Hor. So, then you only married to keep a whore to yourself.

'Do women of honour drink and sing bawdy songs?' Quack asks, and is answered, 'O, amongst friends, amongst friends', and later on we see them at it. He throws his venom at the very audiences: says Sparkish:

I go to a play as to a country treat: I carry my own wine to one, and my own wit to t'other, or else I am sure I should not be merry at either. And the reason why we are often louder than the players is, because we think we speak more wit, and so become the poet's rivals in his audience: for to tell the truth, we hate the silly rogues; nay, so much, that we find fault even with their bawdy upon the stage, while we talk nothing else in the pit as loud.

But it is wonderfully good once Wycherley overcomes his hatred, and gives free play to the impact of his stage personalities, real living beings, if distorted. How his tremendous laughter bears everything before it! Listen to Horner making his confession to Lady Fidget. How easily, how naturally, he handles a complete reversal of outwardly accepted social values!

Lady F. But, poor gentleman, could you be so generous, so truly a man of honour, as for the sakes of us women of honour, to cause yourself to be reported no man? No man! and to suffer yourself the greatest shame that could fall upon a man, that none might fall upon us women by your conversation? but, indeed, sir, (are you) as perfectly, perfectly the same man as before your going into France, sir? as perfectly, perfectly, sir?

Horner. As perfectly, perfectly, madam. Nay, I scorn you should take my word; I desire to be tried only, madam.

Lady F. Well, that's spoken again like a man of honour: all men of honour desire to come to the test. But, indeed, generally you men report such things of yourselves, one does not know how or whom to believe; and it is come to that pass, we dare not take your words, no more than your tailor's, without some staid servant of yours be bound with you. But I have so strong a faith in your honour, dear, dear, noble sir, that I'd forfeit mine for yours, at any time, dear sir.

Horner. No, madam, you should not need to forfeit it for me; I have given you security already to save you harmless, my late reputation being so well known in the world, madam.

Lady F. But if upon any future falling-out, or upon a suspicion of my taking the trust out of your hands, to employ some other, you, yourself should betray your trust, dear sir? I mean, if you'll give me leave to speak obscenely, you might tell, dear sir.

Horner. If I did, nobody would believe me. The reputation of impotency is as hardly recovered again in the world as that of cowardice, dear Madam.

Lady F. Nay, then, as one may say, you may do your worst, dear, dear sir.

Lady Fidget, indeed, is masterly, and gives opportunities for the most intense ridicule:

Sir Jasper. Stay, stay; faith, to tell you the naked truth—
Lady Fidget. Fy, Sir Jasper! do not use that word naked.

There is, moreover, a passage in this play that reveals the whole of that social problem characteristic of the period, or rather exhibits the sort of thing to which the attempt to rationalize sex may, and in that period did, come. Jealous

Pinchwife has just left the room, and Lady Fidget, Mrs. Squeamish, and Mrs. Dainty are left alone.

Mrs. Squeam. Here's an example of jealousy!

Lady Fid. Indeed, as the world goes, I wonder there are no more jealous, since wives are so neglected.

Mrs. Dainty. Pshaw! as the world goes, to what end should they be jealous?

Lady Fid. Foh! 'tis a nasty world.

Mrs. Squeam. That men of parts, great acquaintance, and quality, should take up with and spend themselves and fortunes in keeping little playhouse creatures, foh!

Lady Fid. Nay! that women of understanding, great acquaintance, and good quality, should fall a-keeping too of little creatures, foh!

Mrs. Squeam. Why, 'tis the men of quality's fault; they never visit women of honour and reputation as they used to do; and have not so much as common civility for ladies of our rank, but use us with the same indifferency and ill-breeding as if we were all married to 'em.

Lady Fid. She says true; 'tis an arrant shame women of quality should be so slighted; methinks birth—birth should go for something; I have known men admired, courted, and followed for their titles only.

Mrs. Squeam. Ay, one would think men of honour should not love, no more than marry out of their own rank.

Mrs. Dainty. Fy, fy, upon 'em! they are come to think cross breeding for themselves best, as well as for their dogs and horses.

Lady Fid. They are dogs and horses for't.

Mrs. Squeam. One would think, if not for love, for vanity a little.

Mrs. Dainty. Nay, they do satisfy their vanity upon us sometimes; and are kind to us in their report, tell all the world they lie with us.

Lady Fid. Damned rascals, that we should be only wronged by 'em! To report a man has had a person, when he has not had a person, is the greatest wrong in the whole world that can be done to a person.

Mrs. Squeam. Well, 'tis an arrant shame noble persons should be so wronged and neglected.

Lady Fid. But still 'tis an arranter shame for a noble person to neglect her honour, and defame her own noble person with little inconsiderable fellows, foh!

Mrs. Dainty. I suppose the crime against our honour is the same with a man of quality as with another.

Lady Fid. How! no sure, the man of quality is likest one's husband, and therefore the fault should be the less.

Mrs. Dainty. But then the pleasure should be the less.

Lady Fid. Fy, fy, fy, for shame, sister! whither shall we ramble? Be continent in your discourse, or I shall hate you.

Mrs. Dainty. Besides, an intrigue is so much the more notorious for the man's quality.

Mrs. Squeam. 'Tis true that nobody takes notice of a private man, and therefore with him 'tis more secret; and the crime's the less when 'tis not known.

Lady Fid. You say true, i' faith, I think you are in the right on't: 'tis not an injury to a husband, till it be an injury to our honours; so that a woman of honour loses no honour with a private person; and to say truth——

Mrs. Dainty. So the little fellow is grown a private person—with her——(*Apart to* MRS. SQUEAMISH.)

Lady Fid. But still my dear, dear honour——

Enter SIR JASPER, HORNER, *etc.*

Sir Jasper. Ay, my dear, dear of honour, thou hast still so much honour in thy mouth——

Horner. That she has none elsewhere. (*Aside.*)

The actual *Country Wife* portions are not so good as the rest, perhaps because they were borrowed. There is not the conviction about Pinchwife—a rather too simplified Arnolphe—nor the reality about Mrs. Margery that vivify Horner, the Fidgets, Squeamish, and their set. The scenes are certainly sparkling with vigour and movement, full, even too full, of masterly stage effects, but somehow they are not so creatively conceived as the rest. The moral hangs too obviously upon them, and Wycherley drives it home at the expense of art. Nevertheless the whole thing is carried on with vast gusto; a torrent of life rushes through the play, so that the railing passages cease to be railing, and become part of the picture in which humanity is unfalteringly portrayed. The puppets seem now and again to show a human face, and 'while we cross his vociferous stage, the curious and unholy men and women who hurtle against us seem living beings'.* Wycherley was still the moralist, but the moralist has become caught up in the artist. *The Country Wife* is a complete thing in itself.

The play caused a certain uproar; it struck too closely home, for it was probably, as Steele said, 'good representation of the age in which that comedy was written'. Evidently, to judge by the prefatory quotation, it drew criticism on account of that 'strangeness in the proportion' Bacon tells us is one of the essentials of a work of art. 'I am out of patience', again Wycherley quoted from Horace, 'when anything is blamed, not because it is thought coarsely or inelegantly composed, but because it is new.' But the main attack was on another ground, and the real defence is contained in *The Plain Dealer*.

It is an appeal to fact. 'You pretend to be shocked', Wycherley argued in effect, 'at the representation on the stage of things you practice in everyday life. You are vile wretches that have not even the grace to be honest.' It is interesting to contrast the atmosphere with that of the *Critique de l'École des Femmes*, where the same theme is treated.

> *Olivia.* Then you think a woman modest that sees the hideous *Country Wife* without blushing, or publishing her detestation of it? D'ye hear him, cousin?
> *Eliza.* Yes, and am, I must confess, something of his opinion; and think, that as an over-conscious fool at a play, by endeavouring to show the author's want of wit, exposes his own to more censure, so may a lady call her own modesty in question, by publicly cavilling with the poet's. For all these grimaces of honour and artificial modesty disparage a woman's real virtue,

* Mr. Gosse.

as much as the use of white and red does the natural complexion; and you must use it very, very little, if you would have it thought your own.

Olivia. Then you would have a woman of honour with passive looks, ears, and tongue, undergo all the hideous obscenity she hears at nasty plays.

Eliza. Truly, I think a woman betrays her want of modesty, by showing it publicly in the playhouse, as much as a man shows his want of courage by a quarrel there; for the truly modest and stout say least, and are the least exceptious, especially in public.

Olivia. O, hideous, cousin! this cannot be your opinion. But you are one of those who have the confidence to pardon the filthy play.

Eliza. Why, what is there ill in't, say you?

Olivia. O, fy, fy, fy! would you put me to the blush anew? call my blood into my face again? But to satisfy you then; fisrt, the clandestine obscenity in the very name of Horner.

Eliza. Truly, 'tis so hidden, I cannot find it out, I confess.

There is certainly no *clandestine* meaning in the name; it was most appropriate, and needed no defence. But the passage becomes really ludicrous at the end. The china is made as portentous as the abominable ' Et ' of the *Critique de l'École des Femmes*. We must remember that to get china was the excuse the ladies made for going to Horner's rooms, so Olivia's remarks are not without point.

Olivia. I say, the lewdest, filthiest thing is his china; nay, I will never forgive the beastly author his china. He has quite taken away the reputation of poor china itself, and sullied the most innocent and pretty furniture of a lady's chamber; insomuch that I was fain to break all my defiled vessels. You see, I have none left; nor you, I hope.

Eliza. You'll pardon me, I cannot think the worse of my china for that of the playhouse.

Olivia. Why, you will not keep any now, sure! 'Tis now as unfit an ornament for a lady's chamber as the pictures that come from Italy and other hot countries; as appears by their nudities, which I always cover, or scratch out, as soon as I find 'em. But china! out upon it, filthy china, nasty, debauched china.

Taken with the context, especially with Olivia's general behaviour, Wycherley's attitude is unmistakable. Lamb's defence would have seemed to him not merely the utmost frivolity, but the gravest insult.

The reply, one will say, is common sense, as it ought to be in critical comedy, but this is not really the stuff of which Wycherley was made. If he preached the happy mean, it was only by accident. In the end perhaps, not thinking it possible, or even desirable, he merely wished people to be more honest. That certainly would seem to be the implication of *The Plain Dealer*. ' Yet take this advice with you in this plain-dealing age, to leave off forswearing yourself; for when people hardly think the better of a woman for her real modesty, why should you put that great constraint upon yourself to feign it?' Common sense again, yes, but it must be a common sense as hard as flint; one must be absolute in this too. All compromise is unbearable.

What are we finally to make of Wycherley? or rather, what are we to make of his masterpiece, *The Country Wife*? Somehow he has conquered life, overcome all that he loathed in it, and moulded it into a work of art. But his immense attraction for the sordid was not like that of Dostoievsky, for whom the passionate spirit in man redeemed everything. None of Wycherley's beings reach out at anything beyond immediate actuality, they have no metaphysic. They are curious symbols out of which, by some hard quality of will, he was able to make an artistic gem. It exists, it adds something to our emotions, to our knowledge, and to our aesthetic experience. Wycherley would not be subdued to what he worked in, and he achieved his result by means of not critical, but philosophic, laughter. But what a struggle it was to get there!

His figures, with their bursting vitality, their writhing

in what is at once their power and their impotence, remind us not of Moliere's but of Webster's. They have all the malignancy, all the *naïveté*, but not the flashes of pity. There is nothing like, ' Cover her face, mine eyes dazzle, she died young '. Nor is there the self-pity. There is no ' Thou art a fool then, to waste thy pity on a thing so wretched as cannot pity itself '. But there is much of their defiance, with this difference; Webster's men and women are defiant because they will not submit, Wycherley's because they have submitted.

In his first plays we see Wycherley coldly, disdainfully, a little fearfully, poking with his finger the strange, crawling heap he saw the world to be. But a man such as he was could not stay at that point always; there is too much desire for a clear issue. In *The Plain Dealer* we see him shuddering on the brink; had he the courage to see life face to face without interposing barriers of rage? There is no doubt about *The Country Wife*; there he leaped in with a triumphant laugh. Once again Wycherley had dared.

VII

DRYDEN AND SHADWELL

ADMIRERS of Dryden may be shocked at the treatment of him in the same chapter as Shadwell: but it is for purposes of contrast that they may usefully be bracketed. Langbaine, writing of Shadwell, said, 'I like his comedies better than Mr. Dryden's, as having more variety of characters, and those drawn from the life—I mean men's converse and manners—and not from other men's ideas, copied out of their public writings'. But these very reasons immediately show Dryden to have been the better writer, for he clove to the idea, whereas Shadwell only gave the outward seeming of men in comedy that professed to be purely humouristic. Yet in one important respect they remain alike as writers of comedy: they saw life from no particular angle. Both accepted simply and unaffectedly the attitude of their day, and invoked common sense to repress exaggerations which made life uncomfortable. But there the likeness ends.

DRYDEN.

Born 1631.
The Wild Gallant, 1663.
Sir Martin Mar-all, 1667.
Marriage à la Mode, 1672.
Limberham, 1678.
Amphitryon, 1690.
Died, 1700.

If we cannot rank Dryden as a very great imaginative artist, as a man of letters he is a giant. He lives in the popular mind chiefly as a satirist, as the forerunner and the equal of Pope, yet he was never the aggressor in controversy. When attacked he struck to slay outright, not from any malice, but because whatever he set himself to do, he did with all his vigour. For the rest he was unfailingly generous, almost too humbly so, wherever he saw real merit.

The truth is he was not much interested in life, he cared nothing for politics, and probably not much for religion. One guesses that he conformed to the changing opinions of his day—until change itself became ridiculous—because he wanted to be left alone to pursue his dominating, his unique interest, literature. To reform the language, to search for the key to the house of great art, there was his life.

' Dryden may be properly considered as the father of English criticism,' Johnson said, and this is true—but we must remember that Johnson could have no conception of what criticism was to become in the hands of a Lamb, a Pater, or a Santayana. Thus Dryden's criticism is in no sense an attempt to approach the artist, or even the work of art; it is an attempt to penetrate to the mysteries of art itself, not of course metaphysically, but structurally. Thus he is the writers' critic, *par excellence,* and as such will always be valuable. His grand mistake, from the modern point of view, was in considering not so much what a work of art was, as what it ought to be; but we love his work for the manner of its doing, which is incomparable, and itself great art.

His thirst for correctness in poetic language—'he found it brick and left it marble'—led him, however, into some strange errors of misunderstanding. Compare in *Troilus and Cressida*; 'The specialty of rule hath been neglected' (Shakespeare) with 'The observance due to rule hath been neglected' (Dryden), to take a single instance, where the very sense of the speech is altered by the substitution of one word for another. But it does not follow that because he altered *Troilus*, and *The Tempest*, and *Antony and Cleopatra*, that he produced inferior Shakespeare plays; he made something different because he wanted another thing. One may compare *Antony and Cleopatra* with *All for Love*, as Verrall did so brilliantly, confessing it was 'not much to the purpose', but they are not to be balanced against each other in the same scale, for different forms of art are incommensurable.

Dryden, together with his age, did not, could not, appreciate what Shakespeare was trying to do; yet Dryden is the author of one of the finest panegyrics upon him in our language. And if he loved Ben Jonson well this side idolatry, he gave sound reasons for his criticism. His epistle dedicatory to *Amphitryon* reveals his steady sense of proportion: 'Were this comedy wholly mine, I should call it a trifle . . . but when the names of Plautus and Molière are join'd in it, that is, the greatest names of ancient and modern comedy, I must not presume so far on their reputation, to think their best and most unquestioned productions can be termed little.' For if Dryden's mind was not profound, it was extraordinarily acute and well-balanced, and for all his 'improvements' of the language, for all his vast learning, which he wore so easily and distributed with so little pedantry, he realized that in his own works and in those of his contemporaries, something was missing. Although his was 'a much better age than the last—I mean for versification and the art of numbers . . . in the drama we have not arrived to the pitch of Shakespeare and Ben Jonson' (Dedication to *Examen Poeticum*).

He confessed that playwriting did not come easily to him, but his immense critical skill, in default of high creative capacity, enabled him to forge work of very pure metal. Indeed, one might say of him what he said of Ovid, 'everything which he does, becomes him . . . our poet has always the goal in his eye, which directs him in his race: some beautiful design, which he first establishes, and then contrives the means, which will naturally conduct it to his end'. And since everything he did he did well, when he came to write comedy, once he had cleared up his method he saw exactly what he wanted to do, and did it with amazing directness. In one sense the whole idea of Restoration comedy is summed up in the opening song of *Marriage à la Mode*:

> Why should a foolish Marriage Vow,
>   Which long ago was made,
> Oblige us to each other now,
>   When Passion is decay'd?
> We lov'd, and we lov'd, as long as we cou'd:
>   'Till our love was lov'd out in us both:
> But our Marriage is dead, when the Pleasure is fled:
>   'Twas Pleasure first made it an Oath.
>
> If I have Pleasures for a Friend,
>   And farther Love in store,
> What wrong has he, whose Joys did end,
>   And who cou'd give no more?
>   'Tis a Madness that he
>   Should be jealous of me,
>   Or that I shou'd bar him of another:
>   For all we can gain,
>   Is to give ourselves Pain,
>   When neither can hinder the other.

The rest of the play consists in variations on this theme, and there could be no clearer statement of Restoration assumptions, or, in the unfolding of the plot, a more brilliant *résumé* of what happened when men tried to act upon those assumptions. How witty it is! How enthrallingly amusing! for he always touched the exact spot where the shoe pinched.

To discuss all Dryden's work would take too much space, and moreover his earlier comedies are confused in idea, and even clumsy—although in his second piece he could deal such a delightful stroke as 'children of whom old parents tell such tedious tales'. He is at his best in the polished as opposed to the naturalistic comedy of manners (how dull *Limberham* is!), where he could work to the full his conviction that 'repartee was the charm of conversation, and the soul of comedy'. So although *Sir Martin Mar-all, The Spanish Friar*, and *Amphitryon* have strong claims, we may confine ourselves to the comedy scenes of *Marriage à la Mode*, since it is the type of all Restoration comedy served up in Dryden's most flavoured sauce. Yet, curiously, one is made to feel that Dryden had a contempt for this 'artificial' comedy, writing as he did in the prologue:

> We'll follow the new mode which they begin,
> And treat 'em with a room, and couch within;
> For that's one way, howe'er the play fall short,
> T' oblige the Town, the City, and the Court,

as though to say, 'Very well, if you want the sex duel, stuff like *She Would if She Could, The Amorous Prince* (Behn), or *The Sullen Lovers*, you shall have it; I can do it as well as anybody if I try', and in brilliant anticipation of his successors, his style does not fall very far short of the polished antitheses of Congreve, while in the treatment of marriage quarrels he forestalls Vanbrugh. He has not the free joyousness of Etherege nor the power of Wycherley, but he shows a talent equal to theirs, if he has no special comic flavour to impart to his use of it. His essence, after all, is in his diction: accepting the duel of the sexes as his main theme, he made the most of it he could.

The plot of *Marriage à la Mode* is roughly this: Palamede returns to his native ' Sicily ' from a five years' grand tour, and meets Doralice, with whom he immediately falls in love. To his annoyance he finds that she is the wife of his great friend Rhodophil. No matter, a married man has no rights; he must look to his own. Rhodophil, on the other hand, is in love with Melantha, to whom Palamede's parents are contracting him in marriage. Well, Rhodophil must hasten so as to bring matters to a satisfactory conclusion before his friend marries his mistress. Although Rhodophil and Palamede would now be enemies, they have to assume friendship for the sake of easier access to their hoped-for mistresses. Doralice is quite ready to deceive her husband, while Melantha, whose sole ambition is to be one of the inner circle at Court, is indifferent. But in spite of many attempts, Palamede never succeeds in his plots, and is married to Melantha before Rhodophil has gained his end. Lust is baffled and the marriage tie unviolated, and the friends agree to live together in amity, not, of course, from an ethical motive, but because otherwise life becomes so troublesome and uneasy. Dryden here is the perfect example of the writer of critical comedy, though in this case the moral is, ' J'aime mieux une vertu commode qu'un vice fatigant '.

Every argument in favour of extra-marital relationships is brought forward with extraordinary wit, the arguments surely used by every wild gallant of those days, but as surely never so pithily stated. But Dryden did not think it possible

to rationalize sex; he knew that love involved jealousy.
' Yet I must marry another,' Palamede says, ' and yet I
must love this: and if it leads me into some little incon-
veniences, as jealousies, and duels, and death, and so forth;
yet while sweet love is in the case, Fortune do thy worst!'
And Dryden is careful to show that jealousy can be a very
grave little inconvenience. But at first all seems to go well,
for Rhodophil tells Palamede, ' The greatest misfortune
imaginable is fallen upon me'; he is married, wretchedly
married, to a lady he admits is young, gay, and beautiful
—at least he confesses people say so, but how can he tell?
' Ask those, who have smelt to a strong perfume two years
together, what 's the scent?'

> *Rhodophil.* All that I know of her perfections now, is only by
> memory; I remember, indeed, that about two years ago I
> loved her passionately; but those golden days are gone, Pala-
> mede. Yet I loved her a whole half year, double the natural
> term of any mistress, and think in my conscience I could have
> held out another quarter, but then the world began to laugh at
> me, and a certain shame of being out of fashion, seized me. At
> last, we arrived at that point, that there was nothing left in us
> to make us new to one another. . . .
>
> *Palamede.* The truth is, your disease is very desperate; but
> though you cannot be cured, you may be patched up a little;
> you must get you a mistress, Rhodophil; that, indeed, is living
> upon cordials; but, as fast as one fails, you must supply it with
> another. You're like a gamester, who has lost his estate; yet
> in doing that, you have learned the advantages of play, and can
> arrive to live upon 't.
>
> *Rhodophil.* Truth is, I have been thinking on't, and have just
> resolved to take your counsel,

and the cordial he had in his eye was Palamede's betrothed
lady, Melantha. He ' could e'en wish it were his wife
Palamede loved, when he finds he is to be married to his
mistress'. An easy, a fashionable thing to say, but it does
not work out quite so nicely in actuality.

Nothing, of course, must be left to the imagination, or to mere description. We have heard that Rhodophil and Doralice are loving in public, and quarrel in private. So we are first shown them behaving like a pair of turtles, Rhodophil vowing that 'I have been married above these two years, and find myself every day worse and worse in love. Nothing but madness can be the end on't.' Then, when the witness of conjugal affection has gone, we have a scene which Vanbrugh was later to take as a model for his best passages, but which he scarcely equalled:

Rho. What, is she gone?

Dor. Yes; and without taking leave.

Rho. Then there's enough for this time. (*Parting from her.*)

Dor. Yes, sure, the scene's done, I take it.

(*They walk contrary ways on the stage; he, with his hands in his pockets, whistling; she, singing a dull, melancholy tune.*)

Rho. Pox o' your dull tune, a man can't think for you.

Dor. Pox o' your damn'd whistling; you can neither be company to me yourself, nor leave me to the freedom of my own fancy.

Rho. Well, thou art the most provoking wife!

Dor. Well, thou art the dullest husband, thou art never to be provoked.

Rho. I was never thought dull, till I married thee; and now thou hast made an old knife of me, thou hast whetted me so long, till I have no edge left.

Dor. I see you are in the husband's fashion; you reserve all your good humour for your mistresses, and keep your ill for your wives.

Rho. Prithee leave me to my own cogitations; I am thinking over all my sins, to find for which of them it was I married thee.

Dor. Whatever your sin was, mine's the punishment.

Rho. My comfort is, thou art not immortal; and when that blessed, that divine day comes of thy departure, I'm resolved I'll make one Holy-day more in the almanac, for thy sake.

Dor. Ay, you had need make a Holy-day for me, for I'm sure you have made me a martyr.

Rho. Then, setting my victorious foot upon thy head, in the first hour of thy silence, (that is, the first hour thou art dead, for I despair of it before), I will swear by thy ghost, an oath as terrible to me as *Styx* is to the gods, never more to be in danger of the banes of matrimony.

Dor. And I am resolved to marry the very same day thou diest, if it be but to show how little I'm concerned for thee.

Rho. Prithee, Doralice, why do we quarrel thus a-days? ha? this is but a kind of heathenish life, and does not answer the ends of marriage.

But, human nature being what it is, there is no help for it.

Rho. If only thou could'st make my enjoying thee but a little less easy, or a little more unlawful, thou should'st see what a termagant lover I would prove. . . .

Dor. Well, since thou art a husband, and wilt be a husband, I'll try if I can find out another! 'Tis a pretty time we women have on't, to be made widows, while we are married. Our husbands think it reasonable to complain, that we are the same, and the same to them, when we have more reason to complain, that they are not the same to us.

How admirably to the point it all is!

It is of no use to try to give an idea of the explosive fun of the intrigue; the scenes in the shrubbery, and in the inn —where the ladies are disguised as boys—are certainly unsurpassed in any comedy for sheer amusement. To read them is to laugh aloud, to see them acted is to make the sides ache. Collier may have found them licentious, but in Dryden there is always so direct, so virile a quality, that the word 'filth' cannot be applied. There is health and sanity in every phrase. But let us turn to the conclusion.

Doralice renounced Palamede: she will not have a married man for a lover. She will 'invade no property', and besides, 'a married man is but a mistress's half-servant'. She does not deny Palamede's statement that 'married people can never oblige each other, for all they do is duty, and consequently there can be no thanks', but there is no help for it, and she is deaf to Palamede's repeated sighs—'If we had but once enjoyed one another'; but then the thought comes to him, 'But then once only is worse than not at all; it leaves a man with such a lingering after it'. 'The only way to keep us new to one another', Doralice says, 'is never to enjoy, as they keep grapes, by hanging 'em upon a line; they must touch nothing if you would preserve 'em fresh.' But the retort to that is, 'then they wither and grow dry in the very keeping'. There seems to be no satisfactory solution to the problem, but . . . if Doralice outlives Rhodophil—! And if Palamede outlives Melantha—!

When Rhodophil and Palamede come together, at last armed with the knowledge of each other's doings, they clap their hands on the hilts of their swords, and Dryden brings the common sense argument to bear on Restoration assumptions with a light skill he never surpassed:

Dor. Hold, hold; are not you two a couple of mad fighting fools, to cut one another's throats for nothing?

Pal. How for nothing? He courts the woman I must marry.

Rho. And he courts you whom I have married.

Dor. But you can neither of you be jealous of what you love not.

Rho. Faith I am jealous, and that makes me partly suspect that I love you better than I thought.

Dor. Pish! a mere jealousy of honour.

Rho. Gad, I am afraid there's something else in 't; for Palamede has wit, and if he loves you, there's something more in ye than I have found; some rich mine, that I have not yet discovered.

Pal. 'Slife, what's this? Here's an argument for me to love Melantha; for he has loved her, and he has wit, too, and for aught I know there may be a mine; but if there be, I'm resolved to dig for 't.

Dor. (To RHODOPHIL.) Then I have found my account in raising your jealousy: O! 'tis the most delicate sharp sauce to a cloyed stomach, it will give you a new edge, Rhodophil.

Rho. And a new point, too, Doralice, if I could be sure thou art honest.

Dor. If you are wise, believe me for your own sake; love and religion have but one thing to trust to; that's a good sound faith.

But still, there is something so attractive in the rational argument, that Palamede cannot give up without a struggle:

Pal. What dost think of a blessed community betwixt us four, for the solace of the women, and relief of the men? Methinks it would be a pleasant kind of life: wife and husband for the standing dish, and mistress and gallant for the dessert.

Rho. But suppose the wife and the mistress should both long for the standing dish, how should they be satisfied together?

Pal. In such a case they must draw lots: and yet that would not do neither; for they would both be wishing for the longest cut.

Rho. Then I think, Palamede, we had as good make a firm league, not to invade each other's property.

Pal. Content, say I. From henceforth all acts of hostility cease betwixt us.

Thus Dryden laughs morality back into its rightful place, as the scheme which ultimately makes life most comfortable.

This play is also famous for the character of Melantha, the Frenchified feminine fop, who haunts the court, ' and thinks herself undone, if she be not seen three or four times a day, with the Princess Amalthea '. And in spite of Dryden's modest confession that he felt himself unsuited to write plays, to have produced so actable a character shows that he had overcome all his difficulties. The performance of the part by the beautiful and charming Mrs. Verbruggen forms the subject of what is the best written of all Cibber's paragraphs:

Melantha is as finished an impertinent as ever flutter'd in a drawing room, and seems to contain the most complete system of female foppery that could possibly be crowded into the tortured form of a fine lady. Her language, dress, motion, manners, soul, and body, are in a continual hurry to be something more than is necessary or commendable. . . . She reads the letter [Palamede brings from his father] with a careless, dropping lip, and an erected brow, humming it hastily over, as if she were impatient to outgo her father's commands, by making a complete conquest of him at once; and that the letter might not embarrass her attack, crack! she crumbles it at once into her palm, and pours upon him her whole artillery of airs, eyes and motion; down goes her dainty, diving body, to the ground, as if she were sinking under the conscious load of her own attractions; then launches into a flood of fine language, and compliment, still playing her chest forward in fifty falls and risings, like a swan upon waving water; and, to complete her impatience, she is so rapidly fond of her own wit, that she will not give her lover leave to praise it. Silent assenting bows, and vain endeavours to speak, are all the share of conversation he is admitted to, which, at last, he is relieved from by her engagement to half a score visits, which she *swims* from him to make, with a promise to return in a twinkling.

But what is a fine lady without the final polish of French phrases? These must be gathered by her maid, and learned in a morning's study:

Melantha. O, are you there, Minion? And, well, are not you a most precious damsel, to retard all my visits for want of language, when you know you are paid so well for furnishing me with new words for my daily conversation? Let me die, if I have not run the risk already, to speak like one of the vulgar; and if I have one phrase left in all my store that is not threadbare and *usé*, and fit for nothing but to be thrown to peasants.

Philotis. Indeed, Madam, I have been very diligent in my vocation; but you have so drained all the French plays and romances, that they are not able to supply you with words for your daily expence.

Mel. Drained? What a word's there! *Épuisée*, you sot you. Come, produce your morning's work.

Phil. 'Tis here, Madam. (*Shows the paper.*)

Mel. O, my Venus! fourteen or fifteen words to serve me a whole day. Let me die, at this rate I cannot last till night. Come, read your words; twenty to one half of 'em will not pass muster.

Phil. (Reads) *Sottises.*

Mel. Sottises; bon. That's an excellent word to begin withal; as for example; he, or she, said a thousand *sottises* to me. Proceed.

Phil. Figure: as what a *figure* of a man is there! *Naïve* and *naïveté*.

Mel. Naïve! as how?

Phil. Speaking of a thing that was naturally said; it was so *naïve*; or such an innocent piece of simplicity; 'twas such a *naïveté*.

Mel. Truce with your interpretations; make haste.

Phil. Faible, Chagrin, Grimace, Embarrasse, Double Entendre, Équivoque, Éclaircissement, Suite, Bévue, Façon, Penchant, Coup d'étourdi, and *Ridicule.*

Mel. Hold, hold, how did they begin?

Phil. They began at *Sottises,* and ended *en Ridicule.*

Mel. Now give me your paper in my hand, and hold you my glass, while I practise my postures for the day. (MELANTHA *laughs in the glass.*) How does that laugh become my face?

Phil. Sovereignly well, Madam.

Mel. Sovereignly? Let me die, that's not amiss. That word shall not be yours: I'll invent it, and bring it up myself. My new point gorget shall be yours upon't. Not a word of the word, I charge you.

Phil. I am dumb, Madam.

Mel. That glance, how suits it with my face?

Phil. 'Tis so *languissant.*

Mel. Languissant! That word shall be mine too, and my last Indian gown thine for it.

and to conclude matters, Rhodophil's *billet doux* is so French, so *galant* and so *tendre*, that she cannot resist the temptation of a tryst.

SHADWELL

Born 1640.
The Sullen Lovers, 1668.
The Humourists, 1670.
The True Widow, 1679.
The Lancashire Witch and *Teague O' Dively*, 1681.
The Squire of Alsatia, 1688.
The Scowrers, 1690.
Died, 1692.

To turn from material of this quality to Shadwell's effu-
sions is to exchange an Epicurean meal for the dishes of
a countryman at his Christmas jollification. It is good
enough fare, nourishing no doubt, but heavy, and the
sweetmeats are of the nature of bullseyes. Instead of sparkling wine, there is beer, and though old October would be
welcome enough, Shadwell only provides us with swipes;
however we cannot complain of the quantity.

It is interesting, nevertheless, to compare the works of
two men who seem to have had much the same point of
view in life, who as far as fable and moral go appear to say
much the same thing, and who produce something totally
different yet of the same kind. Neither has anything startling to communicate in the way of ideas: the whole difference lies in the manner, for whereas Dryden's fine virility
and good taste produced solid works of art, Shadwell's
dullness defeated even laughter. In truth, as Dryden said,
his rival could ' do anything but write '. Hasty Shadwell,
who ' scorned to varnish his good touches o'er ', had, in
contrast with Dryden's avowed costiveness, a fatal facility
which forbad distinction in word or phrase. He often said
things not worth while, he was prolix and prosy, clumsy
and flabby; he had certainly not learned the final art, the
art to blot. Wycherley rightly said of him that, ' he knew
how to start a fool very well, but was never able to run him

down'. One feels of Dryden that he was a literary athlete in superb training, whereas Shadwell was over-fleshed, and breathed heavily after a very short span of exercise. He is often amusing, but never gives those flashes of revelation that are the essence of the dramatic in comedy as well as in tragedy.

Yet it is not quite true to say he had no individual style, for his passages are immediately recognizable. To take one from *The Virtuoso*:

> *Clarinda.* A sot, that has spent £2,000 in microscopes, to find out the nature of eels in vinegar, mites in a cheese, and the blue of plums which he has subtilely found out to be living creatures.
>
> *Miranda.* One who has broken his brains about the nature of maggots, who has studied these twenty years to find out the several sorts of spiders, and never cares for understanding mankind.

There is a kind of pudding-like quality that is unmistakable.

It is difficult to speak of his plays; they have almost every conceivable fault from the literary point of view; they are exaggerated and clumsy, or, flat and stale, the commonplace expression of a commonplace man. It was not fair to say that he was ' in the realms of nonsense absolute ', for his work bears the impress of the dullest sense. The humours are infinitely worried, driven home by blow after badly aimed blow. In *The Sullen Lovers*, a travesty of *Les Fâcheux*, a whole act is devoted to the excesses of Sir Positive At-all to end with the following:

> *Sir Positive.* Hold, hold, hold, hold! Navigation, geography, astronomy, palmistry, physic, divinity, surgery, ¦ arithmetic, logic, cookery, and magic: I'll speak to every one of these in their order. If I don't understand 'em every one in perfection, nay, if I don't fence, dance, ride, sing, fight a duel, speak French, command an army, play on the violin, bagpipe, organ, harp, hautboy, sackbut, and double curtal, speak Spanish, Italian,

Greek, Hebrew, Dutch, Welsh and Irish, dance a jig, throw the bar, swear, drink, swagger, whore, quarrel, cuff, break windows, manage affairs of state, hunt, hawk, shoot, angle, play at cat, stool-ball, scotch hop and trap-ball, preach, dispute, make speeches—(*coughs*). Prithee get me a glass of small beer, Roger.

Stanford. Hell and furies !

Emilia. Oh ! Oh !   (*They run.*)

Sir. Pos. Nay, hold, I have not told you half ; if I don't do all these and fifty times more, I am the greatest owl, pimp, monkey, jackanapes, baboon, rascal, oaf, ignoramus, logger-head, cur-dog, blockhead, buffoon, jack-pudding, tony, or what you will. Spit upon me, kick me, cuff me, lug me by the ears, pull me by the nose, tread upon me and despise me more, than the world now values me.

(*Exeunt omnes, and he goes out talking as fast as he can.*)

There is little art here ; yet at the same time, if one expects no very high level, and is content to be mildly amused without any mental exertion, one may pass the time very pleasantly with Og. His plays have the sort of action that tells upon the stage in a farcical way. *Bury Fair* is a pleasant enough fancy, if the humours are rather obvious and often derivative. *The Squire of Alsatia* has a broad Middletonian bustle that quite submerges the moral that youth should be allowed to have his fling lest worse befall, and gives in its stead a certain sensation of life. It is founded on the *Adelphoe* of Terence. As a preacher of the golden mean Shadwell, however, failed to be convincing because he accepted too placidly the already quoted motto of Mercury in Molière's *Amphitryon* ;

> J'aime mieux un vice commode
> Qu'une fatigante vertu,

so that his would-be criticism of humours and ' acquired follies ' scarcely has point. ' Faith, ma'am, I am a moral man ; I do as I would be done by ', is as far as his vision goes. He most certainly believed that comedy has a moral purpose, but if the comic dramatist is to achieve this object, he must illuminate life from a point of view a little superior to the ordinary. He must be able to generalize, and this Shadwell could not do. He laughed only at those at whom everybody laughed ; the bore, the fop, the gallant, the light lady, the pompous pedant, and so on. He gave the outward appearance of a person, but never the idea behind, so that no knowledge of the human heart is added to us by a perusal of his plays.

But through this very defect, he has the great merit of reproducing the manners of his time, the manners, not of the polished exquisites, but of the everyday men and women of the period. London life is brought whole upon the stage, not only in bourgeois types, but also in ruffians, who do battle with the forces of law and order. His ' What play do they play ? Some confounded play or other ', is admirable realism, and even in his own day he was regarded as a living gazette of manners. Thus Etherege wrote from Ratisbon, ' Pray let Will Richards send me Mr. Shadwell's (play) when it is printed, that I may learn what follies are in fashion '.

He had great talent, but no literary sense, an eye for a situation (which after all, does not make high comedy), but no real ability to treat it. He ' promised a play and dwindled to a farce '. Yet, if he borrowed from others, others sometimes found it worth while to borrow from him, though in the latter case the improvement is more marked than complimentary. He was popular in his own day, and that may be allowed to count for something. If he is never trenchant, he is sometimes acute. In *A True Widow*, when Lump refers contemptuously to men of pleasure as men not fond of business, Lady Cheatly replies, ' So fools say, who seem to be excellent men of business, because they always make a business of what is none ; and seem to be always very industrious because they take great pains for what a witty man does with ease '. This, however, is on the

higher level of his observations. In spite of the usual prefer-
ence for *Bury Fair*, *A True Widow* is possibly his best play,
though even there the poppy hangs about his brow. It has
a greater purposefulness that his other plays—he never could
reach an airy carelessness—and more of the 'judgement'
Dryden required. Besides, the humours are, in one or two
instances, more lightly handled. Young Maggot really induces
laughter, not too common in some of his sixteen works:

> *Bellamour.* A man must use exercise to keep himself down;
> he will belly else, and the ladies will not like him.
> *Young Mag.* I have another way to bring down my belly.
> *Stanford.* Another? What's that?
> *Young Mag.* Why, I study; I study and write. 'Tis exercise
> of the mind does it. I have none of the worst shapes or com-
> plexions. 'Tis writing and inventing does my business. . . . I
> have an engine to weigh myself when I sit down to write or
> think, and when I unbend myself again.
> *Prig.* How do you unbend?
> *Young Mag.* Why, I unbend my imagination, my intellect. . . .

This play was rather unaccountably damned, perhaps because, like Dryden's *Limberham*, it exposed the 'crying sin
of Keeping'. But indeed, there is very little of exposure,
and the keeper undergoes no discomfort in either play. In
any case, Restoration audiences were used to being lashed
upon this point, and would not be scared away by any
frankness of treatment. If one may hazard a reason, it is
that the public at large, then as to-day, loved a touch of
romance, and this is lacking in both plays. Critical fun and
frolic may make up for its absence with an intelligent audience, but if both elements are absent, woe betide the piece.

Shadwell was made Laureate at the Revolution, vice
Dryden, Roman Catholic, and he died in 1692, just as the
man who was to show the immense value of the proper use
of words was rising to his full glory, and giving final point
to subject-matter at the existence of which Shadwell had
scarcely guessed.

VIII

CONGREVE

Born 1670.
The Old Bachelor, 1693.
The Double Dealer, 1693.
Love for Love, 1695.
The Way of the World, 1700.
Died, 1729.

THERE can hardly be another instance to put beside
Congreve of a man who sprang so immediately to the
pinnacle of literary fame, and, if we make due allowance for
the natural exaggeration of his contemporaries, has ever
since maintained his position so inalienably. It is true that
no one to-day would attempt to rank him with Shakespeare,
as Dryden did in the well-known lines:

Heaven, that but once was prodigal before,
To Shakespeare gave as much; she could not give him more,

but compared with others, who have been likened to our
eternal poet, Congreve has held his place with reasonable
stability. The critics of the early nineteenth century were
loud in his praises; Lamb gave him his full due, and even
Macaulay could not withhold his admiration. Only Leigh
Hunt tempered his enthusiasm, perhaps merely to balance
Hazlitt's fine tribute. *The Way of the World*, the latter
wrote, 'is an essence almost too fine, and the sense of
pleasure evaporates in an aspiration after something that
seems too exquisite ever to have been realized'. This is the
true note, struck by Hazlitt with his faculty of seeing more
clearly than any of his contemporaries, and of seeing things

separately. He was the first, apart from the men of Congreve's day, to realize him as a poet, with a poet's longing for beauty. Other critics have failed to see that the masterly style accomplishes something other than a clear exposition of manners. So Coleridge wrote, ' Wickedness is no subject for comedy. This was Congreve's great error and peculiar to him. The dramatic personalities of Dryden, Wycherley, and others are often viciously indecent, but not like Congreve's, wicked.' Again, Leigh Hunt remarked, ' We see nothing but a set of heartless fine ladies and gentlemen coming in and going out, saying witty things at each other, and buzzing in some maze of intrigue '. To Mr. Gosse, the exquisite wording reveals no more than satire, and a ' careless superiority '. Congreve's brilliance, indeed, is so dazzling, that admiration nearly always stops short at praising it, and fails to perceive the real force of the man, the solid personality, and the knowledge of human beings. So Macaulay of his epigram: ' In this sort of jewelry he attained to a mastery unprecedented and inimitable,' and Henley—' He is saved from oblivion by the sheer strength of style.' Meredith's famous passage is in the same vein : ' He hits the mean of a fine style and a natural in dialogue. He is at once precise and voluble. . . . In this he is a classic, and is worthy of treading a measure with Molière.' Mr. Whibley praises him for economy, as ' a stern castigator of prose '. ' In point and concision, his style is still unmatched in the literature of England. There is never a word too much, or an epithet that is superfluous.'

These praises are abundantly warranted, but too great an attention to style in this sense is apt to obscure the broader vision. A brilliant technique, of which verbal style is a part, is developed through the impulsion to express something, and it is in relation to this that style must be considered.

If we read Congreve sympathetically we must admit that a comedy for him was not a mere game, but like every other good piece of writing, ' the precious life blood of a master spirit embalmed and treasured up on purpose to a life beyond life '. Congreve, indeed, had rather more to say than the mode he chose for speech would allow him; and one may suspect that it was the realization of this, combined with the failure of *The Way of the World*, that made him abandon the stage at the age of thirty.

Born ten years after the Restoration, he came to maturity after the Revolution. Times were becoming more stable, and men could look back upon the life of the last thirty years with something of detachment. The attempt to rationalize sexual relations had by now definitely failed, as may be judged by the outbursts against women, such as Rochester's *Satyr against Marriage*, and Gould's *Satyrs against Women and against Wooing*, all of which were published at the time Congreve was writing. Collier was raising his voice; the age of reason, of Steele and Addison, was at hand. Congreve stands midway between the ages, with a temper as balanced as the couplets of Pope.

' Two kinds of ambition early took possession of his mind,' Macaulay observed, ' and often pulled it in opposite directions.... He longed to be a great writer. He longed to be a man of fashion.... The history of his life is the history of a conflict between these two impulses.' But, at bottom, the impulse was the same. A man of undoubted sensibility, he was always seeking the finest quality in everything, in life as well as in writing. It is this which constitutes him a poet. His well-known remark to Voltaire that he wished to be visited ' upon no other foot than that of a gentleman who led a life of plainness and simplicity ', was no idle affectation. In any case one could pardon his irritation against a lion-hunting little Frenchman who had as yet written nothing very important, and who came to see him, not for what he was, but for what he had been more than twenty years before! But besides that he really did think it more worthy to be a gentleman than a wit, seeing that to be a wit involved so great a degradation of humanity. ' Those characters which are meant to be ridiculed in most of our comedies,' he wrote, in the dedication of *The Way of the World*, ' are of fools so gross, that in my humble opinion, they should rather disturb than divert the well-natured and reflecting part of an audience; they are rather objects of charity than contempt; and instead of moving our mirth, they ought very often to excite our compassion '. A bitter confession from a comic writer who, moreover, preferred, as he wrote to Keally, to ' feel very sensibly and silently for those whom I love ', and who said in a letter to Dennis, ' I profess myself an enemy to detraction. . . . I never care for seeing things that force me to entertain low thoughts of my nature. . . . I could never look long upon a monkey without very mortifying reflections.' Finally, he was one of the three ' most honest hearted, real good men, of the poetical members of the Kit-Cat Club '.

So, as one reads his first three comedies, one feels all the time that he is at war with himself. He has the technical brilliance of style, the rapier wit, the lively antithesis that no one can surpass, but not always that real style which is the complete fusion of manner and words with the artist's ' sense of fact '. For perfect expression the artist must be expressing himself, and this, one feels, Congreve was not always doing. Perhaps only Etherege could in this kind, and he never wearied as Congreve sometimes seems to do. The light-hearted atmosphere was not really natural to him, for he had something of Jonson and Wycherley about him.

Yet he was Wycherley with a difference, a Wycherley who did not hate the people about whom he wrote so much as pity them. If he despised some of them, he only showed it to the extent that a gentle nature would permit. Etherege in a sense sings, Wycherley is all imprecation, but Congreve is a constructive thinker. If he had too much culture for the brutality of Wycherley and too much sympathy for the irony of Jonson, he had too much knowledge for the airy light-heartedness of Etherege. All the time, behind the coldly critical surface, there is much of the poet, of the man hungry for beauty. There is often a caressing touch, and Millamant he must really have loved. There are even moments when one wonders if he is not going to crash his comic structure to pieces with some passionate outburst. He might be saying with Stendhal, 'Je fais tous les efforts possibles pour être sec. . . . Je tremble toujours de n'avoir écrit qu'un soupir, quand je crois avoir noté une vérité.'

From the opening lines of *The Old Bachelor* we are in the realm of ideas, and realize that we are in contact with a thinker.

> *Bellmour.* Business!—and so must time, my friend, be close pursued, or lost. Business is the rub of life, perverts our aim, casts off the bias, and leaves us wide and short of the intended mark.
>
> *Vainlove.* Pleasure, I guess, you mean.
>
> *Bel.* Ay, what else has meaning?
>
> *Vain.* Oh, the wise will tell you—
>
> *Bel.* More than they believe—or understand.
>
> *Vain.* How, how, Ned, a wise man say more than he understands?
>
> *Bel.* Ay, ay; wisdom's nothing but a pretending to know and believe more than we really do. You read but of one wise man, and all that he knew was, that he knew nothing.

The thought is not very profound—who would expect Bellmour to be profound? 'leave wisdom to fools, they have need of it', he says—but it shows well enough that Congreve's 'humours' were to be intellectual rather than bodily.

Heartwell, the old bachelor himself, is animated by a real comic idea. He is a man who, in spite of all his efforts, is drawn to women, hating and despising himself for it, but unable to fight against the impulse. We find him in front of the lodging of Silvia, who attracts him so much, that he finds, to his great disgust, that he is willing to marry her. He soliloquizes :

> Why whither in the devil's name am I a-going now ? Hum— let me think—is not this Silvia's house, the cave of that enchant- ress, and which consequently I ought to shun as I would infec- tion ?   To enter here, is to put on the envenomed shirt, to run into the embraces of a fever, and in some raving fit, be led to plunge myself into that more consuming fire, a woman's arms. Ha ! well recollected, I will recover my reason and begone. . . . Well, why do you not move ? Feet do your office—not one inch ; no, foregad I'm caught !—There stands my North, and thither my needle points.—Now could I curse myself, yet cannot repent. O thou delicious, damn'd, dear, destructive woman !

This variant of Launcelot Gobbo is not only ludicrous in the extreme, it is profound. It strikes at the deepest dis- harmonies in man's nature, and touches that bedrock of discordant impulses, in the face of which, if we cannot ignore, we must either laugh or perish.

There is already something of Congreve's final excellence in Bellmour and Belinda, precursors of Mirabell and Milla- mant. Here we have sex antagonism in full blast, the realism touched with just the necessary lightness and delicacy :

> *Belinda.* (*Interrupting* BELLMOUR.) Prithee, hold thy tongue— Lard, he has so pestered me with flames and stuff—-I think I shan't endure the sight of a fire this twelvemonth.
> *Bellmour.* Yet all can't melt that cruel frozen heart.

Belinda. O gad, I hate your hideous faney—you said that once before—If you must talk impertinently, for heaven's sake let it be with variety ; don't come always, like the devil, wrapped in flames—I'll not hear a sentence more, that begins with an ' I burn '—or an ' I beseech you, madam '.

On the other hand, the Heartwell–Silvia scenes have none of this charming fencing ; frank statement takes its place. ' If you love me you must marry me ', gives the true picture of Silvia's directness.

The Fondlewife scenes, which are irrelevant to the plot, fall from the height of comedy to erotics and buffoonery, although Fondlewife himself has a hint of Jonson's Kitely ; like him he fears to go to business lest he should be cuckolded in his absence. The pimping valet Setter has some of the earthy philosophy Calderon, Regnard and Beaumarchais knew how to give their servants, and this Congreve probably derived from Terence. But the bawdy scenes are simply dull comedy of intrigue, and the Nykin-Cocky dialogues reach a level of realism which make them almost as humiliating as the Nicky-Nacky scenes in *Venice Preserved*, though there is none of the degrading filth of the masochistic Antonio.

Congreve's skill as a manipulator of pure frolic is immediately seen ; he could handle farce as well as anybody. The timid Sir Joseph Wittol, with his cowardly protector, Captain Bluffe, provides unceasing amusement. We are clearly in the realm of Elizabethan comedy, and Bluffe, the braggadocio, has a long ancestry through Bobadil and Parolles to Thraso. The scenes where he appears are admirably rounded off in real fun, with the point driven well home. It is no wonder that Dryden called this the best first play he had ever read.

The next play, *The Double Dealer*, is in many respects puzzling. ' I designed the moral first ', Congreve wrote, 'and to that moral I invented the fable', and he prefixed to the comedy a line from Horace to the effect that 'sometimes even comedy exalts her voice'. There is no doubt about the admirable lucidity of the plot and the ingenuity of the construction. 'I made the plot as strong as I could, because it was single', we are told. So far all is clear, but the difficulty is to arrive at that very subtle and elusive thing, the 'idea' of the play, the dominating mood that led to its creation. This may be conveyed by the action, the delineation of character, or by the atmosphere, which is the resultant of these combined with the wording. And it is in regard to the atmosphere that the curious thing happens. Congreve tried to mingle two distinct and separate worlds, the Charles Lamb world of airy make-believe, and the familiar world of everyday life. Lady Touchwood, indeed, displays passions of which a heroine of Ford need not have been ashamed. 'O I have excuses, thousands for my faults; fire in my temper, passions in my soul, apt to every provocation; oppressed at once with love, and with despair'; and in a later act, 'Oh! that I were fire indeed, that I might burn the vile traitor. What shall I do? how shall I think? I cannot think.' Maskwell also is of this tempestuous world; there is something tremendous about him. He has a cold completeness, an absolute detachment from good, that is masterly, 'For wisdom and honesty, give me cunning and hypocrisy; oh, 'tis such a pleasure, to angle for fair-faced fools', he says, and his ingenious ingenuousness is as daring in conception as it is convincing in the execution. True, he is not very subtle, like all type figures he is not seen in the round, and one cannot conceive him as anything but a villain; he is villainy itself.

And mingling with this harsh world which enables us to understand Leigh Hunt's comment that 'there is a severity of rascality . . . in some of his comedies that produces upon many of their readers far too grave an impression ', we have the world of the Froths, the Plyants, and Brisk. This is the very culmination of social tomfoolery. Listen to Brisk making love to Lady Froth:

> *Lady F.* O be merry by all means—Prince Volscius, in love ! ha ! ha ! ha !
>
> *Brisk.* O barbarous, to turn me into ridicule ! Yet, ha ! ha ! ha !—the deuce take me, I can't help laughing myself, ha ! ha ! ha !—yet by heavens ! I have a violent passion for your lady-ship, seriously.
>
> *Lady F.* Seriously ? ha ! ha ! ha !
>
> *Brisk.* Seriously, ha ! ha ! ha ! Gad, I have, for all I laugh.
>
> *Lady F.* Ha ! ha ! ha !—what d'ye think I laugh at ! Ha ! ha ! ha !
>
> *Brisk.* Me, egad, ha ! ha !
>
> *Lady F.* No, the deuce take me if I don't laugh at myself ; for, hang me ! if I have not a violent passion for Mr. Brisk, ha ! ha ! ha !
>
> *Brisk.* Seriously ?
>
> *Lady F.* Seriously, ha ! ha ! ha !
>
> *Brisk.* That 's well enough ; let me perish, ha ! ha ! ha ! O miraculous ! what a happy discovery ; ah, my dear, charming Lady Froth !
>
> *Lady F.* O my adored Mr. Brisk !   (*They embrace.*)

all in deliberate contrast with the furies of Lady Touchwood or the sensibility of Cynthia.

Congreve himself does not seem to have been quite satisfied with this play, as he confessed in the Epistle Dedicatory ; and he must have realized why it was not that pure comedy he had attempted to create. Omit the three lines spoken at the end by Brisk and Lady Froth, and the play would altogether cease to be critical comedy, and would become something much more dynamic ; it would almost be melodrama. Those remarks, however, bring it back to the static, and make us realize that nothing had really happened. We have Maskwell unmasked, thwarted, consumed by a cold irony; Touchwood in a violent rage casting his wife out of the house; Lady Touchwood in an agony of despair, so that one cannot help being carried away by the dramatic movement. More than the intellectual apparatus is touched, one is borne along by the onrush of life; then suddenly, Brisk—' This is all very surprising, let me perish!' It is like an icy douche, everything is brought to a standstill, and we are once more in the realm of that comedy where none of the emotions are important. It is almost too sudden and drastic; the human spirit is hardly capable of adjusting itself so rapidly. Yet it succeeds on the stage, justification enough for such magnificently daring technique.

It is difficult to see how the Mellefont-Maskwell intrigue can be called comedy. Towards Maskwell and Lady Touchwood Congreve has not the attitude of the comedy writer, nor of the satirist; he is the cold and virtuous wielder of the chastening rod. Neither are Touchwood, Mellefont, or Cynthia figures of critical comedy; their appeal is to our sympathy. They are admirably honest, simple, likeable people, and Cynthia is altogether charming. They do, however, fulfil the purposes of critical comedy in so far as they provide models of the golden mean.

Congreve's wit is not at its deepest in this play, but if it descends too often to the cheap level of the Witwouds rather than aims at that of the Truewits, it is always light and spinning. It is worthy of Brisk, but not of Mellefont or Careless. One may, it is true, answer a fool according to his folly, but only if there is the likelihood of his being wise in his own conceit. And this is a little too facile:

> *Brisk.* Careless ... you're always spoiling company by leaving it.

vs spoiling company by coming into 't.
, man! When I say you spoil com-
you leave nobody for the company

arly always magnificently neat and
of fops highly entertaining. Lady
be met with in real life, but here
of comedy. She is, perhaps, most
here she makes advances to the
res nothing for her, but is eager

ws how circumstances may happen
together—To my thinking, now I could resist the strongest
temptation. But yet I know, 'tis impossible for me to know
whether I could or not; there's no certainty in the things of
this life.

Mel. Madam, pray give me leave to ask you one question.

Lady P. O Lord, ask me the question! I'll swear I'll refuse
it! I swear I'll deny it!—therefore don't ask me; nay, you
shan't ask me; I swear I'll deny it. O Gemini, you have brought
all the blood into my face! I warrant I'm as red as a turkey-
cock; O fie, cousin Mellefont.

Mel. Nay, madam, hear me; I mean——

Lady P. Hear you! No, no. I'll deny you first, and hear you
afterwards. For one does not know how one's mind may change
upon hearing. Hearing is one of the senses, and the senses
are fallible; I won't trust my honour, I assure you, my honour
is infallible and uncomatable.

Mel. For Heaven's sake, madam——

Lady P. O name it no more—Bless me, how can you talk of
Heaven! and have so much wickedness in your heart? Maybe
you don't think it a sin.—They say some of you gentlemen
don't think it a sin.—Or . . . . Maybe it is no sin to them that
don't think it so; indeed, if I did not think it a sin.—but still
my honour, if it were no sin.—But then, to marry my daughter,
for the conveniency of frequent opportunities, I'll never consent
to that; as sure as can be, I'll break the match.

Here we reach levels Wycherley could barely guess at. It
is indeed being voluble as well as precise, and is really

comic if comedy is concerned with the antics of the human being caught in the social net. Moreover, the characterization is clearly drawn in the dialogue. Each character speaks with his or her own authentic voice, and has an outside existence.

Work which aims at the quality after which Congreve was striving is not to be produced hurriedly, and his next work, *Love for Love*, shows traces of carelessness. It is often considered to be Congreve's best play, and was very popular when first acted. But Congreve's best was not for the vulgar, and we can imagine it was the return to a certain Jonsonian obviousness that made *Love for Love* so palatable to the playgoers. It is possible that the treatment of the humours, here so evident, was suggested by the popularity of Wilson's *The Cheats*, which had reached a fourth edition in 1693. Certain passages indicate that the character of Foresight may have been taken from the astrologer Mopus, with this difference, however, that Mopus was a self-professed charlatan, whereas Foresight deluded himself. Again, there are many moments in the play where we think of Wycherley rather than of Congreve. For instance, when Valentine feigning madness says to Tattle, ' My friend, what to do? I am no married man, and thou canst not lie with my wife; I am very poor, and thou canst not borrow money of me; then what employment have I for a friend?', it might be Manly resuscitated.

Congreve seems to have felt that the comic stage was losing some of its force, and that this needed reviving. In this connexion a portion of the prologue is worth quotation :

> We've something too, to gratify ill-nature,
> (If there be any here) and that is satire.
> Though satire scarce does grin, 'tis grown so mild,
> And only shows its teeth, as if it smiled.

As asses thistles, poets mumble wit,
And dare not bite, for fear of being bit.
They hold their pens, as swords are held by fools,
And are afraid to use their own edge-tools.
Since the Plain-Dealer's scenes of Manly rage
No one has dared to lash this crying age.
This time, the poet owns the bold essay. . . .

a sufficient indication of his purpose, and perhaps of his in-
spiration. The position of the poet too, seems to have
occupied Congreve's mind, more, probably, from the need
for effusive and insincere dedications, than from such incidents as Otway's pitiful death from starvation. Says Scandal:

> Turn pimp, flatterer, quack, lawyer, parson, be chaplain to
> an atheist, or stallion to an old woman, anything but a poet;
> a modern poet is worse, more servile, timorous and fawning,
> than any I have named: without you could retrieve the ancient
> honours of the name, recall the stage of Athens, and be allowed
> the force of open, honest satire.

Thus the general tone and the form of this play can be
accounted for. Indeed, Congreve from the first had not been
altogether averse from satire, and could make excellent
thrusts, but his hand was too light for a whole 'essay' in
this kind, and in comparison with his best work, he here
becomes a little tedious, and even repetitive. It follows that
many passages, though they are good Wycherley, are poor
Congreve. We may take as an example Scandal's account
of Tattle:

> A mender of reputations! ay, just as he is a keeper of secrets,
> another virtue that he sets up for in the same manner. For the
> rogue will speak aloud in the posture of a whisper; and deny
> a woman's name, while he gives you the marks of her person; he
> will forswear receiving a letter from her, and at the same time
> show you her hand in the superscription: and yet perhaps he
> has counterfeited the hand too, and sworn to a truth; but he
> hopes not to be believed; and he refuses the reputation of a

lady's favour, as a doctor says No to a bishopric, only that it may be granted him.—In short, he is a public professor of secrecy, and makes proclamation that he holds private intelligence.

This is overweighty, and not only are we forthwith given a scene where, to illustrate the above, Tattle is easily trapped into indiscretions, but the same is repeated in a later act.

The satiric lash is again apparent in the famous Tattle-Prue scene, so different from the same kind of scene as treated by Etherege, quoted in a previous chapter. Prue, we must remember, is an *ingénue* from the country.

> *Prue.* Well; and how will you make love to me? Come, I long to have you begin. Must I make love too? You must tell me how.
>
> *Tat.* You must let me speak, miss, you must not speak first; I must ask you questions, and you must answer.
>
> *Prue.* What, is it like the catechism?—Come then, ask me.
>
> *Tat.* D'ye think you can love me?
>
> *Prue.* Yes.
>
> *Tat.* Pooh! Pox! you must not say yes already; I shan't care a farthing for you then in a twinkling.
>
> *Prue.* What must I say then?
>
> *Tat.* Why, you must say no, or you believe not, or you can't tell—
>
> *Prue.* Why, must I tell a lie then?
>
> *Tat.* Yes, if you'd be well-bred. All well-bred persons lie. Besides, you are a woman, you must never speak what you think; your words must contradict your thoughts: but your actions may contradict your words. So, when I ask you, if you can love me, you must say no, but you must love me too. If I tell you you are handsome, you must deny it, and say I flatter you. But you must think yourself more charming than I speak you; and like me for the beauty which I say you have, as much as if I had it myself. If I ask you to kiss me, you must be angry, but you must not refuse me. If I ask you for more, you must be more angry—but more complying; and as soon as ever I make you say you'll cry out, you must be sure to hold your tongue.

Prue. O Lord, I swear this is pure!—I like it better than our old-fashioned country way of speaking one's mind; and must not you lie too?

Tat. Hm!—yes, but you must believe I speak truth.

Prue. O Gemini! Well, I always had a great mind to tell lies; but they frighted me, and said it was a sin.

Tat. Well, my pretty creature; will you make me happy by giving me a kiss?

Prue. No, indeed, I'm angry at you. (*Runs and kisses him.*)

Tat. Hold, hold, that's pretty well—but you should not have given it me, but have suffered me to have taken it.

Prue. Well, we'll do it again.

Tat. With all my heart.—Now then, my little angel.

(*Kisses her.*)

Prue. Pish!

Tat. That's right—again my charmer!　(*Kisses her again.*)

Prue. O fy! nay, now I can't abide you.

Tat. Admirable! That's as well as if you had been born and bred in Covent Garden.

What follows is as well as if she had been born and bred in some Oriental *wazir*. Yet the whole is certainly trenchant satire, verging upon the venomous, and conformable to the general opinion of women in that age. But it lacks the exquisiteness one has learned to expect from Congreve. He had abandoned the rapier for the bludgeon, as he had abandoned the comedy of manners for the comedy of humours. The equally famous scene between Mrs. Foresight and Mrs. Frail is at a better level.

Mrs. Fo. I suppose you would not go alone to the World's End? [This was a somewhat disreputable tavern.]

Mrs. Fr. The world's end! What! do you mean to banter me?

Mrs. Fo. Poor innocent! you don't know that there's a place called the World's End? I'll swear you can keep your countenance purely, you'd make an admirable player.

Mrs. Fr. I'll swear you have a great deal of confidence, and in my mind too much for the stage.

Mrs. Fo. Very well, that will appear who has most; you were never at the World's End?

Mrs. Fr. No.

Mrs. Fo. You deny it positively to my face?

Mrs. Fr. Your face! What's your face?

Mrs. Fo. No matter for that, it's as good a face as yours.

Mrs. Fr. Not by a dozen years' wearing. But I do deny it positively to your face then.

Mrs. Fo. I'll allow you now to find fault with my face;—for I'll swear your impudence has put me out of countenance;—but look you here now—where did you lose this gold bodkin? O sister, sister! . . .

Mrs. Fr. Well, if you go to that, where did you find this bodkin? O sister, sister!—sister every way.

Such a disclosure serves but to make the sisters friends, for ' ours are but slight flesh wounds, and if we keep 'em from air, not at all dangerous '. A neat statement of a social philosophy not unknown at the present day, while the repartee throughout is as good as the characters demand.

But in this play, in spite of its rather ponderous satire, and the humours of Foresight and Sir Sampson Legend—the latter at times reminiscent of Old Bellair—something of Congreve appears that is peculiarly his own, an expression of longing to find the world finer than it really is, a poetic fastidiousness and a depth of feeling that make him more than any other Englishman akin to Molière. It is already adumbrated in *The Double Dealer*:

Mellefon·. You're thoughtful, Cynthia?

Cynthia. I'm thinking, though marriage makes a man and wife one flesh, it leaves 'em still two fools: and they become more conspicuous by setting off one another.

Mel. That's only when two fools meet, and their follies are opposed.

Cyn. Nay, I have known two wits meet, and by the opposition of their wit, render themselves as ridiculous as fools. 'Tis an odd game we are going to play at; what think you of drawing stakes, and giving over in time?

The fear of lost illusion seems to haunt him. Like Valentine in *Love for Love*, Congreve is melancholy at the thought of

spoiled ideals and spoiled beauty. A passionate ardour for
the finer side of life breathes constantly from his pages.
Valentine for instance says:

> You're a woman—one to whom Heaven gave beauty, when
> it grafted roses on a briar. You are the reflection of heaven in
> a pond, and he that leaps at you is sunk. You are all white, a sheet
> of lovely spotless paper, when you first are born; but you are to
> be scrawled and blotted by every goose's quill. I know you; for I
> loved a woman, and loved her so long, that I found out a strange
> thing; I found out what a woman was good for,

and this was 'to keep a secret; for though she should tell,
yet she is not to be believed'. This is one of Congreve's
'heartless' men; and now for one of his 'heartless' women.
Angelica speaks:

> Would any-thing but a madman complain of uncertainty?
> Uncertainty and expectation are the joys of life. Security is an
> insipid thing, and the overtaking and possessing of a wish,
> discovers the folly of the chase. Never let us know one another
> better; for the pleasure of a masquerade is done, when we
> come to show our faces.

This is not the observation of a jilt, of a baggage without
sensibility, but of a woman who has known and suffered,
who has been disappointed in her early estimate of things.
It is the weary cry of the knower who realizes that happiness may not be sought for or grasped, and that joy must
be snatched as it flies. These were not mere puppets, but
breathing, living, desiring men and women.

Love for Love, indeed, ends on the wistful note, with
Angelica's tender, sad argument, which is a plea for mutual
trust, an almost despairing outburst against the injustice
done her sex:—

> You tax us with injustice, only to cover your own want of
> merit. You would all have the reward of love; but few have
> the constancy to stay till it becomes your due. Men are generally
> hypocrites and infidels, they pretend to worship, but have neither
> zeal nor faith.

The thread of sadness and disillusion runs through these plays, and live passions break through the veil of cynicism wherewith the critical comedy clothes itself. We pierce through the social world to the realm of our underlying motives, to our ardours and desires, for beauty as well as for grosser satisfactions; and Congreve reveals himself as a poet pleading for finer living.

If *Love for Love* is Congreve's best *stage* play, *The Way of the World* is his masterpiece of literary art, as well as his final vindication of mankind. In it glows the true Congreve, the Congreve to whom detraction was wearisome, and who aspired after that very fragile thing, beauty itself.

In reading his dedication and his prologue we are reminded of a Frenchman, not of Molière, however, nor of any one of that century, but of—Flaubert. The aspiration is the same, the dislike of human folly is the same; there is the identical feeling that the highest achievement is the creation of beauty through the quality and texture of words. Congreve does not explicitly mention his aim, but it is implicit in his paragraphs in which he speaks again and again of ʻ purity of style ʼ, and ʻ perfection of dialogue ʼ. This was his great aim, the creation of beauty by plastic means. ʻ Je me souviens ʼ, Flaubert says, ʻ d'avoir eu des battements de cœur, d'avoir ressenti un plaisir violent en contemplant un mur de l'Acropole, un mur tout nu . . . Eh bien ! Je me demande si un livre, indépendamment de ce qu'il dit, ne peut pas produire le même effet.ʼ Surely Congreve too asked himself that question. Like Flaubert, he wrote, not for the mob, but for the *few* (the italics are his own), qualified to distinguish those who write ʻ with care and pains ʼ. ʻ That it succeeded on the stage, was almost beyond my expectation,ʼ and he might have gone on, ʻ car j'écris (Je parle d'un auteur qui se respecte) non pour le lecteur d'aujourd'hui, mais pour tous les lecteurs qui pourront se présenter, tant que la langue vivra'. Like Flaubert, again, he would not meddle between the audience and his presentation of life. He would

> Give you one instance of a passive poet
> Who to your judgements yields all resignation,

for, 'Quant à laisser voir mon opinion personnelle sur les gens que je mets en scène; non, non, mille fois non!' It is this attitude that has led to the popular view of 'the great and splendid Mr. Congreve', the man of 'unruffled temper', the gentleman of 'perfect urbanity'. As though good art ever came out of perfect urbanity!

Thus his poetry, his art, the essential stuff he alone could give, is to be found not so much in the 'fable', or in satire, as in the wording. He was not really interested in his material, and in his dedication envied Terence for having had his subject prepared for him by Menander, so that he could devote his energies to correctness of speech. It is to be remembered that Dryden hailed Congreve as his successor, and that Dryden's great aim was to perfect the language. 'To please, this time, has been his sole pretence,' to 'give delight', in Corneille's and Dryden's sense of the words, with all the beauty of phrase of which he was capable, and thus to express his aspiration after the elusive beauty of humanity. Even on such a commonplace theme as that of sending English fools on the Grand Tour, Congreve could write, ''Tis better to trade with a little loss, than to be quite eaten up with being overstocked'. That is a perfect phrase, concise, but without the least suspicion of a rattle—and marvellous in balance. The vowel-sounds are carefully selected, so that those in the second part of the sentence echo, yet vary without ever repeating, those of the first. That is how poetry is written. A trifling detail, a commonplace remark, it may be said. Possibly : but think of the concentration of artistic purpose that can expend itself on a thing so humble. Certainly this play was not 'prepared for that general taste which seems now to be predominant in the palates of our audience'.

He puts into the mouth of his fool Witwoud a remark Etherege or another might have given to a *jeune premier* : 'A wit should no more be sincere than a woman constant; one argues a decay of parts, as t'other of beauty,' for Congreve hated all this false tomfoolery, this pretence of liking the hateful. But small wonder that the audience was puzzled, and that it was three days before some of the 'hasty judges could find the leisure to distinguish between the character of a Witwoud and a Truewit'. Even Pope, we remember, asked, 'Tell me if Congreve's fools are fools indeed?'

The Way of the World naturally failed at its first appearance on the stage, as it has ever since, except for a short period of partial favour, some thirty years after its birth, when Peg Woffington played Millamant.* Downs said that 'it had not the success the company expected because it was too keen a satire', but in reality, it was too civilized for an age that revelled in the scribblings of Mrs. Pix, and applauded the burlesque of Farquhar's *Love and a Bottle*. But there was also the fact that in many passages Congreve had ceased to write the ordinary comedy. While his secondary characters in his previous plays, his Lord and Lady Froth and his Lady Plyant, are made of that flimsy material which could enable Lamb to call them creatures of a sportive fancy, this is not so with Mrs. Marwood and the Fainalls in this play. Fainall is a repulsive villain, but Mrs. Fainall, whom Mirabell had once loved, is more sinned against than sinning. She remains loyal to Mirabell, and even helps him

* This was written before its success in 1924. Do we grow civilized?

in his advances to Millamant (what profound psychology is here!), but at the same time her heart aches at not being loved by her husband. 'He will willingly dispense with the hearing of one scandalous story, to avoid giving an occasion to make another by being seen to walk with his wife,' she says with an affectation of lightness. But how bitter it is! How full of unnecessary pain is the way of the world!

She and Mrs. Marwood are figures of an intense realism, driven by that insane jealousy which is often more bitter and nearer to the surface in illicit love than in the marriage tie. Mrs. Marwood is Fainall's mistress; but she also loves Mirabell, so that Mrs. Fainall has double reason to be jealous of her; yet it is rather on account of Mirabell she is jealous, and this also is true to life. Fainall, again, is jealous of Mirabell, and goads Mrs. Marwood into a very frenzy of despair, and though all the time he is wounding himself, he cannot resist the impulsion. Never for a moment does the comic penetrate into this tense scene:

> *Fainall.* Will you yet be reconciled to truth and me?
> *Mrs. Marwood.* Impossible. Truth and you are inconsistent: I hate you, and shall for ever.
> *Fain.* For loving you?
> *Mrs. M.* I loathe the name of love after such usage; and next to the guilt with which you would asperse me, I scorn you most. Farewell.
> *Fain.* Nay, we must not part thus.
> *Mrs. M.* Let me go.
> *Fain.* Come, I'm sorry.
> *Mrs. M.* I care not—let me go—break my hands, do—I'd leave 'em to get loose.
> *Fain.* I would not hurt you for the world. Have I no other hold to keep you here?
> *Mrs. M.* Well, I have deserved it all.
> *Fain.* You know I love you.
> *Mrs. M.* Poor dissembling!—O that—well, it is not yet——
> *Fain.* What? what is it not? what is not yet? It is not yet too late.—

Mrs. M. No, it is not yet too late ;—I have that comfort.

Fain. It is, to love another.

Mrs. M. But not to loathe, detest, abhor, mankind, myself, and the whole treacherous world.

Fain. Nay, this is extravagance—Come, I ask your pardon— no tears—I was to blame, I could not love you, and be easy in my doubts. Pray forbear—I believe you ; I'm convinced I've done you wrong ; and any way, every way, make amends. I'll hate my wife, yet more, damn her! I'll part with her, rob her of all she's worth, and we'll retire somewhere, anywhere, to another world. I'll marry thee. Be pacified. 'Sdeath, they come, hide your face, your tears ;—you have a mask, wear it a moment. This way, this way—be persuaded.

To say that these are puppets animated by no real passions is to misunderstand Congreve ; one might as well say the same of Richardson's women.

But he could still be comic when he wished ; take this little inset :

Mirabell. Excellent Foible! Matrimony has made you eloquent in love.

Waitwell. I think she has profited, sir. I think so.

Delicious ridicule ! O complacency of the satisfied male !

But in spite of such passages, in spite of the drunken scenes of Sir Wilful Witwoud and Petulant, and the masquerading of Waitwell as Sir Rowland, which are calculated to appeal to the most stupid elements in an audience, the whole play needs close following sentence by sentence. It is this which makes it everlasting literature. But even that glorious farcical scene between Lady Wishfort and 'Sir Rowland' (IV. xii) is too fine for immediate appreciation. When Lady Wishfort hopes Sir Rowland will not 'impute her complacency to any lethargy of continence', nor think her ' prone to any iteration of nuptials ', or believe that ' the least scruple of carnality is an ingredient ', he assures her, 'Dear Madam, no. You are all camphire and frankincense, all chastity and odour.' On the stage? No, one must repeat it, laughing, to oneself—' all camphire and frankincense, all chastity and odour '. Like good poetry, it speaks to the inward ear.

Although much of this play is the pure presentation of the artist to whom all life is material, and whose attitude towards it must be guessed through the quality of the words rather than by their surface meaning, in the main personages we feel Congreve coming to more direct grips with his inmost self. And the theme in which this is apparent is, inevitably in that age, the theme of love. Millamant, ' Think of her, think of a whirlwind ! ' From the first we know that she and Mirabell really love each other. Mirabell thinks it was for herself she blushed when he blundered into the ' cabal night '; but it was for him, at seeing the man she loved make a fool of himself in company vastly inferior to him. For the first time in his life he is jealous for a woman, ' not of her person, but of her understanding ', and he feels that for a ' discerning man ' he is ' somewhat too passionate a lover; for I like her with all her faults; nay, like her for her faults '. And when they meet, how exquisite they are together, how tenderly she chaffs him :

> *Mirabell.* You are no longer handsome when you've lost your lover; your beauty dies upon the instant: for beauty is the lover's gift; 'tis he bestows your charms—your glass is all a cheat. . . .
> *Millamant.* O the vanity of these men ! . . . Beauty the lover's gift ! Lord ! what is a lover, that it can give ? Why, one makes lovers as fast as one pleases, and they live as long as one pleases, and they die as soon as one pleases ; and then, if one pleases, one makes more.

Mirabell is too serious a lover to take her remarks as fun, or as affectionate teasing; he is goaded into gibes, and although Millamant gets bored with them, she sees the love

behind. But she wants light and air, the freshness of spring
and a clear gaiety—charming, lovable Millamant, no wonder
the young men in the pit would gladly marry her in spite of
Macaulay's sneer—she is the incarnation of happiness, or at
least of the desire for it. 'Sententious Mirabell!—Prithee
don't look with that violent and inflexible wise face, like
Solomon at the dividing of the child in an old tapestry hanging.' Life is serious, but let us at least be gay while we can.

The culmination, of course, is the famous bargaining
scene already referred to. It is Congreve's contribution to
the philosophy of love.

> *Mil.* Ah! don't be impertinent. My dear liberty, shall I
> leave thee? My faithful solitude, my darling contemplation,
> must I bid you then adieu? Ay-h adieu—my morning thoughts,
> agreeable wakings, indolent slumbers, all ye *douceurs*, ye *som-
> meils du matin*, adieu?—I can't do't, 'tis more than impossible—
> positively Mirabell, I'll lie abed in a morning as long as I please.
> *Mir.* Then I'll get up in a morning as early as I please.
> *Mil.* Ah! idle creature, get up when you will—and d'ye
> hear, I won't be called names after I'm married: positively I
> won't be called names.
> *Mir.* Names!
> *Mil.* Ay, as wife, spouse, my dear, joy, jewel, love, sweet-
> heart, and the rest of that nauseous cant, in which men and
> their wives are so fulsomely familiar—I shall never bear that—
> good Mirabell, don't let us be familiar or fond, nor kiss before
> folks, like my Lady Fadler and Sir Francis; nor go to Hyde
> Park together the first Sunday in a new chariot, to provoke
> eyes and whispers; and then never to be seen there together
> again; as if we were proud of one another the first week, and
> ashamed of one another ever after. Let us never visit together,
> nor go to a play together; but let us be as strange as if we had
> been married a great while; and as well bred as if we were
> not married at all.
> *Mir.* Have you any more conditions to offer? Hitherto your
> demands are pretty reasonable.
> *Mil.* Trifles!—As liberty to pay and receive visits to and
> from whom I please; to write and receive letters without

interrogatories or wry faces on your part; to wear what I please; and choose conversation with regard only to my own taste; to have no obligation upon me to converse with wits that I don't like, because they are your acquaintance; or to be intimate with fools because they may be your relations. Come to dinner when I please, dine in my dressing room when I'm out of humour, without giving a reason. To have my closet inviolate; to be the sole empress of my tea-table, which you must never presume to approach without first asking leave. And lastly, wherever I am, you shall always knock at the door before you come in. These articles subscribed, if I continue to endure you a little longer, I may by degrees dwindle into a wife.

Mir. Your bill of fare is something advanced in this latter account. Well, have I liberty to offer conditions—that when you are dwindled into a wife, I may not be beyond measure enlarged into a husband?

Mil. You have free leave; propose your utmost, speak and spare not.

Mir. I thank you. *Imprimis* then, I covenant that your acquaintance be general; that you admit no sworn confidant, or intimate of your own sex; no she friend to screen her affairs under your countenance, and tempt you to make a trial of a mutual secrecy. No decoy-duck to wheedle you a *fop-scrambling* to the play in a mask—then bring you home in a pretended fright, when you think you shall be found out—and rail at me for missing the play, and disappointing the frolic which you had to pick me up and prove my constancy.

Mil. Detestable *imprimis!* I go to the play in a mask!

Mir. *Item*, I article, that you continue to like your own face, as long as I shall: and while it passes current with me, that you endeavour not to new-coin it. To which end, together with all vizards for the day, I prohibit all masks for the night, made of oiled-skins, and I know not what—hog's bones, hares' gall, pig-water, and the marrow of a roasted cat. In short, I forbid all commerce with the gentlewoman in *what d'ye call it* court. *Item*, I shut my doors against all bawds with baskets, and pennyworths of muslin, china, fans, atlasses etc.—*Item*, when you shall be breeding—

Mil. Ah! name it not.

Mir. Which may be presumed with a blessing on our endeavours—

Mil. Odious endeavours!

Mir. I denounce against all strait lacing, squeezing for a shape, till you mould my boy's head like a sugar-loaf, and instead of a man child, make me father to a crooked billet. Lastly, to the dominion of the tea-table I submit—but with *proviso*, that you exceed not in your province ; but restrain yourself to native and simple tea-table drinks, as tea, chocolate and coffee ; as likewise to genuine and authorized tea-table talk—such as mending of fashions, spoiling reputations, railing at absent friends, and so forth—but that on no account you encroach upon the men's prerogative, and presume to drink healths, or toast fellows ; for prevention of which I banish all foreign forces, all auxiliaries to the tea-table, as orange brandy, all aniseed, cinnamon, citron, and Barbadoes waters, together with ratafia, and the most noble spirit of clary—but for cowslip wine, poppy water, and all dormitives, those I allow. These *provisos* admitted, in other things I may prove a tractable and complying husband.

Mil. O horrid *provisos* ! filthy strong waters ! I toast fellows ! odious men ! I hate your odious *provisos* !

And this is commonly considered the behaviour of an arrant coquette ! In reality it is a vision of the conflict in all marriage, of the desire to maintain one's own personality fighting vainly with the desire to love whole-heartedly. Her appeal has all the earnestness of real life about it ; it is vocal of all the hopes and fears of lovers when they see the bright face of happiness tarnished with the shadow of possible disillusion. It *must* not happen that they are very proud of one another the first week, and ashamed of one another ever after. Each of them has seen the rocks which bring most marriages to ruin, and will strive to avoid them. And this to Thackeray was 'a weary feast, that banquet of wit where no love is !'

Not to see this passionate side of Congreve is to lose the best in him ; it is like reading Shakespeare to find that he does not conform to classical rules. For Millamant is a woman ; she has the inestimable power of giving, but she is rightly jealous of herself, and is not to be undervalued. She is alive and breathing, hiding a real personality behind the only too necessary artifices of her sex. Once assured of Mirabell's love, she divests herself of her armour, and shows a perfect frankness. Meredith, in giving Congreve praise for the portraiture, does not do her justice; she is only a 'flashing portrait, and a type of the superior ladies who do not think, not of those who do'. Millamant not think! when on the face of it she has thought a great deal, and thought very clearly, about the living of her own life. She needed to be certain of Mirabell before taking the plunge and dwindling into a wife, for she had all the fastidiousness of a woman of experience. 'If Mirabell should not make a good husband, I am a lost thing.'

The only other figure at all comparable to Millamant is Lady Wishfort, but she is not in the round, and her presentation too nearly approaches satire. 'Her flow of boudoir Billingsgate', says Meredith, 'is unmatched for the vigour and pointedness of the tongue. It spins along with a final ring, like the voice of Nature in a fury, and is indeed the racy eloquence of the educated fishwife.'

Lady Wishfort. No news of Foible yet?

Peg. No, madam.

Lady W. I have no more patience.—If I have not fretted myself till I am pale again, there's no veracity in me! Fetch me the red—the red, do you hear, sweetheart? An arrant ash colour, as I'm a person! Why dost thou not fetch me a little red? Didst thou not hear me, Mopus?

Peg. The red ratafia does your ladyship mean, or the cherry brandy?

Lady W. Ratafia, fool! no, fool. Not the ratafia, fool—grant me patience! I mean the Spanish paper, idiot—complexion, darling. Paint, paint, paint, dost thou understand that, changeling, dangling thy hands like bobbins before thee? Why does thou not stir, puppet? thou wooden thing upon wires!

Her *De Arte Amandi* passage ripples along with un-thinkable skill. After scolding Mirabell, 'Frippery! Super-annuated frippery! I'll frippery the villain!' she turns to a more agreeable subject.

> *Lady W.* But art thou sure Sir Rowland will not fail to come? or will he not fail when he does come? Will he be importunate, Foible, and push? For if he should not be impor-tunate,—I shall never break decorums—I shall die with confu-sion, if I am forced to advance!—I shall swoon if he should expect advances. No, I hope Sir Rowland is better bred, than to put a lady to the necessity of breaking her forms. I won't be too coy, neither—I won't give him despair—but a little disdain is not amiss; a little scorn is alluring.
>
> *Foible.* A little scorn becomes your ladyship.
>
> *Lady W.* Yes, but tenderness becomes me best—a sort of dyingness—you see that picture has a sort of a—ha, Foible! a swimmingness in the eyes—yes, I'll look so—my niece affects it; but she wants features. Is Sir Rowland handsome? Let my toilet be removed—I'll dress above. I'll receive Sir Rowland here. Is he handsome? Don't answer me. I won't know: I'll be surprised. I'll be taken by surprise.
>
> *Foible.* By storm, madam, Sir Rowland's a brisk man.
>
> *Lady W.* Is he! O then he'll importune, if he's a brisk man. I shall save decorums if Sir Rowland importunes. I have a mortal terror at the apprehension of offending against decorums.

Yet such a current of sympathy seems to flow from Con-greve even into this subject, that she becomes almost pathetic, and one feels a touch of the tragic mingled with the comic vision.

The *dénouement* is forced, a mere trumped up affair, but it does not matter, any more than it matters with Tartufe. With the exposure of Fainall, and the emotional torture of Mrs. Marwood, the atmosphere seems almost irretrievably ruined; but then we have,

> *Millamant.* Why does not the man take me? Would you have me give myself to you over again?
>
> *Mirabell.* Ay, and over and over again,

so that the whole torrential scene dissolves before us into grace, and clear, straightforward feeling. When the first rush has gone, one can only gasp at the incomparable art.

Congreve had much of the classical writer of comedy about him; he preached the happy mean. His 'wicked' *jeunes premiers*, and to a less degree his *premières*, are gentlemen and ladies. Bellmour, Mellefont, Valentine, and Mirabell, if their manners are not quite ours—but indeed they are little removed—are never underhand or malicious, and have generosity. Cynthia, Angelica, and Millamant are charming women, warm-hearted, companionable, and direct. These are not scandal-mongers and sharpers, nor would-be wits and heartless jades. They show up in solid relief against the dizzy world of Restoration comedy. It is true that the men are not righteous overmuch; they represent the common-sense attitude current even in Victorian days, they sowed their wild oats. But once they have come to marriage, they show the utmost sincerity. Congreve, however, never saw beyond this. It would never occur to him that an Alceste might, after all, be right. One does not feel with him, as one does with Molière, that the ideal of the *honnête homme* is perhaps not the final philosophy of every-day life. At the same time one sees that his standard would be far above the average in sensibility.

If to refine upon existence was Congreve's dominant desire, as it would appear, there was no more for him to do in the world of comedy. He had tried to invest it with the delicacy of drawing-room poetry, and had failed. The medium of critical comedy was not suitable, and his appeal was to a circle more exquisite than an audience. He was tired of portraying fools and rascals, and the bodily lusts of men and women; and, indeed, the garb of the comic writer never sat altogether easily upon his sensitive shoulders.

Thus, in spite of his excelling qualities, one must confess failure, if we judge by the greatest standards. His criticism never won through to a broader vision; his disillusion conquered him. Too much a poet to accept the surface of life, he was too little a poet to find beauty in the bare facts of existence; and one cannot help regarding him a little as a tragic figure. If, as he believed, it was the duty of the comic poet to lash the vices and follies of humankind, in view of the nature of man it hardly seemed worth while. And as for the creation of beauty, when, after great travail it was achieved, it went unrecognized, and all that the critics could say of it was to call it 'too keen a satire'. Was it not better to sport in the shade with the Amaryllis of social wit, or—with the tangles of a Bracegirdle's hair?

IX

VANBRUGH AND FARQUHAR

VANBRUGH.

Born 1664.
The Relapse, 1696 (sequel to Cibber's *Love's Last Shift*).
Aesop, 1697 (from *Ésope* of Boursault).
The Provok'd Wife, 1697.
The False Friend, 1702 (from Le Sage and y Zorrilla).
The Country House, 1703 (?) (from Dancourt).
The Confederacy, 1705 (from Dancourt).
A Journey to London, unfinished at his death.
Died 1726.

CAPTAIN, afterwards Sir John Vanbrugh, Clarencieux King at Arms, architect of Blenheim and many other houses, builder and manager of the Opera House in the Haymarket, was, as can be guessed from his multifarious life, above all things a man of the world, but a very simple and honest man of the world who did things as they came to his hand to do. As one might expect from his versatility, what he chiefly had to bring to the writing of plays was an abundant vigour, to which he added the common sense which earned him a nickname. As literary artist he is as unlike Congreve as can be imagined, but like him he was one of the three ' most honest-hearted real good men, of the poetical members of the Kit-Cat Club ', the third being the obese, generous, and sceptical Dr. Samuel Garth.

Vanbrugh had one valuable requisite of the writer of critical comedy, a contempt for all cant and humbug ; but he failed to be anything of a poet because he had no peculiar vision, and thus his plays can add nothing either to our knowledge of life, or to our aesthetic experience. He presented life as he saw it, but he saw it no differently from the hundred and one other people with whom he daily mingled. Thus if there is no vinegar in his comedies, neither is there any salt. He never for a moment took his audiences away from the life they saw around them (except in a few passages, especially in his first comedy, that approach burlesque), nor did he show it from any particular angle. He probably took his comedies no more seriously or strenuously than he took life; both for him were a matter of easy adaptation, a little rough and tumble, and a great deal of good luck. He put down naturally what occurred to him easily, with the result that his comedy, as Congreve remarked of Cibber's *Love's Last Shift*, 'had only a great many things that were like wit, that in reality were not wit'.

But he had more than a little sense of the stage. He knew what would be effective, and we follow his plays with the amusement we feel at all evasions, and at revelations of the cunning in humanity. In all his works it is the plot that matters, and he put the moral second. That he confessed fondness for a moral when driven to make some statement we have seen in an earlier chapter, and this is further shown by his adaptation of Boursault's *Ésope*. Yet in *The Relapse*, the interest is clearly not in the 'problem' play of Loveless, Amanda, and Berinthia, as the title would imply, nor even in the character of Lord Foppington, but in the story of Tom Fashion outwitting his brother, and carrying off the heiress Hoyden. Collier was quite right when he said the play should have been called *The Younger Brother or The Fortunate Cheat*. Indeed, his only idea in writing the play,

and not a bad one either, was to divert the gentlemen of
the town, if possible, ' and make them forget their spleen
in spite of their wives and taxes '.

His originality consisted in breathing the spirit of
Middleton or Massinger into the works of his French and
English contemporaries. He accepted their plays and the
conventions of his time, but altered, and it must be confessed, spoiled them. He never saw what the others were
at, nor knew what he was doing, and he was genuinely
surprised when accused of profaneness and immorality.
Where he was frankly late Elizabethan, as in the scene
between Sir John Brute and the justice, or when he shows
us Sir Tunbelly Clumsey, he is full of vitality, and blows
a breezy atmosphere into life. But this is the end of his
originality. As the list of his plays shows, he found it more
pleasant to adapt than to create, and even in his original
productions he is derivative. Continually, in little sentences,
we catch a reminiscence of an older writer, not only de-
spoiled but ruined. Again and again we are reminded of
other characters or incidents ; the parson in *The Relapse*
reminds us of the parson in *The Cheats*, or of Busy in
Bartholomew Fair. Lady Fanciful in *The Provok'd Wife* is a
revival of Dryden's Melantha ; while in *The Confederacy*,
Dick's surrender of his ring reminds us forcibly of Alderman
Gripe's relinquishment of his in Wycherley's *Love in a
Wood*.

These borrowings would not matter, had he, like Congreve who borrowed freely, improved upon his originals ;
but he had not the lightness of touch, the sureness of point,
the racy descriptiveness of his predecessors. We may take
a few instances of his pilferings, not of course to convict
him, but to make a critical comparison. We have quoted a
passage from *The Old Bachelor*, showing Heartwell in front

of Silvia's door. This is Heartfree, Vanbrugh's version of the misogynist, in *The Provok'd Wife* :

> What the plague ails me?—Love? No, I thank you for that, my heart's rock still.—Yet 'tis Belinda that disturbs me ; that's positive—Well, what of all that? Must I love her for being troublesome?

and so on for some lines. Belinda, again, now and then takes a hint from her sister in Congreve :

> For when a man is really in love, he looks so insufferably silly, that tho' a woman liked him well enough before, she has then much ado to endure the sight of him.

Congreve's young woman has said :

> Could you but see with my eyes, the buffoonery of one scene of address, a lover, set out with all his equipages and appurtenances ; O gad!

The latter is vivid, the former commonplace. Thus *The Confederacy* is full of reminiscences of Congreve, but the delight, the exquisite touch, is lacking. In *The Confederacy* we read of Brass giving a letter to Flippanta for her mistress, and a turn is provided, not by the French author, but by the creator of *The Way of the World*. When she receives the missive, Flippanta asks, ' Are there any verses in it?' and Brass assures her that there is ' not one word in prose, it's dated in rhyme '. This might be amusing if there were no higher standard to make it seem flat, but we cannot help remembering Millamant :

> *Millamant.* I am persecuted with letters—I hate letters— Nobody knows how to write letters ; and yet one has 'em, one does not know why. They serve one to pin up one's hair.
> *Witwoud.* Is that the way? Pray, madam, do you pin up your hair with all your letters? I find I must keep copies.
> *Mil.* Only with those in verse, Mr. Witwoud. I never pin up my hair with prose—I think I tried once, Mincing.
> *Min.* O Mem, I shall never forget it.
> *Mil.* Ay, poor Mincing tift and tift all the morning.

And if all the joy is gone, so is all the philosophy, all the poetry if you will. We may remember Angelica's wistful remark quoted in the last chapter (see page 137) and compare it with a like utterance by Clarissa:

> I always know what I lack, but I am never pleased with what I have. The want of a thing is perplexing enough, but the possession of it is intolerable.

Vanbrugh is full of high spirits, fun, and frolic; but his plays express no desire, the light of the intellect does not illuminate them; in a word, he lacked creative capacity.

It is claimed for him that his dialogue is brisk and easy. 'There is something', Cibber said, 'so catching to the ear, so easy to the memory, in all he writ, that it has been observed by all the actors of my time, that the style of no author whatsoever gave their memory less trouble.' A little consideration shows this to be something of a left-handed compliment, for what is so easy to learn may not be worth the learning. Dialogue, 'so easy to the memory' often degenerates into stuff like this passage from *The Relapse*:

> *Amanda.* Why, do you then resolve you 'll never marry?
> *Berinthia.* O no; I resolve I will.
> *Aman.* How so?
> *Ber.* That I never may.
> *Aman.* You banter me.
> *Ber.* Indeed I don't. But I consider I'm a woman, and form my resolutions accordingly.
> *Aman.* Well, my opinion is, form what resolution you will, matrimony will be the end on 't.
> *Ber.* Faith, it won't.
> *Aman.* How d' you know?
> *Ber.* I'm sure on 't.
> *Aman.* Why, do you think 'tis impossible for you to fall in love?
> *Ber.* No.

Aman. Nay, but to grow so passionately fond, that nothing but the man you love can give you rest?

Ber. Well, what then?

Aman. Why, then you'll marry him.

Ber. How do you know that?

Aman. Why, what can you do else?

Ber. Nothing, but sit and cry.

Aman. Psha!

This is wretched either as life or as art, yet it is not the worst passage deliberately selected. His repartee seldom gets home: if we say that Wycherley used a bludgeon, and Congreve a rapier, we may continue the metaphor and say that Vanbrugh gives us many a lively bout at singlesticks; his personages even come to actual blows on more occasions than one. But he has happy passages, and can claim to have created one character, Lord Foppington. If not quite delicate enough for fantasy, erring too much on the side of exaggeration, yet Lord Foppington succeeds in convincing by consistency with himself. Neither Leigh Hunt who called him ' the quintessence of nullification ', nor Hazlitt who wrote of him as ' the personification of the foppery and folly of dress and appearance in full feather ', quite do him justice. For at bottom he is a very sound man of business, and it is this that makes him a creation of Vanbrugh's and not a mere imitation of Sir Fopling, Sir Courtly, and Sir Novelty. He deliberately aims at absurdity because it pays, and he is proud to be the leader of the coxcombs because they form ' so prevailing a party '. All this is well carried out. One never knows what he is going to say, but once spoken, one realizes it is the only thing he could have said. His argument against reading has cogency; ' Far to my mind the inside of a book, is to entertain one's self with the forc'd product of another man's brain. Naw I think a man of quality and breeding may be much diverted with the natural sprauts of his own.' His behaviour when he finds himself cheated of his heiress is exemplary :

> Naw, for my part, I think the wisest thing a man can do with an aching heart, is to put on a serene countenance ; for a philosaphical air is the most becoming thing in the warld to the face of a person of quality ; I will therefore bear my disgrace like a great man, and let the people see I am above an affrant.

The motives may not be of the highest, but they will serve for a ' nice marality '.

Now and again, as in Lord Foppington's presence, we feel that had Vanbrugh taken the trouble, he might have written good comedy. But on the one hand he was too good-natured for critical comedy, and on the other he lacked the depth of perception to write any other. He confused his values even too much for what he was doing. For instance, he thought he was treating sex exactly as Congreve did, but with him love is no longer a battle of the wits, but a struggle of desire against conscience. The persons of his plays commit adultery with the full knowledge that they are acting contrary to their own morality, and in consequence there is sometimes an atmosphere of lasciviousness which destroys the comic.

Berinthia's surrender to Loveless is a sufficient example. His plays abound in platitudes on sexual morality, and he has been praised for his line, ' To be capable of loving one, is better than to possess a thousand '. But this is not the comic way of inculcating a moral, and thus on the whole his plays make for cuckoldry rather than for continence. The question does not arise with Congreve, but with Vanbrugh it is important, for it shows that he was not sure enough of his attitude to write comedy, which needs at least clarity of outlook.

Indeed there are passages in *The Provok'd Wife* that might

without incongruity have fitted into Lillo's *The London Merchant*. One is even led to think that Vanbrugh's real gift was for domestic drama. Cibber was right when he said ' that his most entertaining scenes seem'd to be no more than his common conversation committed to paper ', and his husband and wife quarrel scenes have a realism which gives the whole atmosphere of dull hopelessness of such scenes in real life :

> *Lady Brute.* Do you dine at home to-day, Sir John ?
>
> *Sir John.* Why, do you expect I should tell you what I don't know myself ?
>
> *Lady Brute.* I thought there was no harm in asking you.
>
> *Sir John.* If thinking wrong were an excuse for impertinence, women might be justified in most things they say or do.
>
> *Lady Brute.* I'm sorry I have said anything to displease you.
>
> *Sir John.* Sorrow for things past is of as little importance to me, as my dining at home or abroad ought to be to you.

It is all a little vulgar as compared with Dryden or Congreve, and the scene ends with a cheap cliché :

> *Lady Brute.* What is it disturbs you ?
>
> *Sir John.* A parson.
>
> *Lady Brute.* Why, what has he done to you ?
>
> *Sir John.* He has married me.

But after all, this was his first attempt at that kind of scene, and there is a much better one in *A Journey to London*, which if finished, would have given him a much higher place in our literature than he actually holds.

> *Lady Arabella.* Well, look you, my Lord, I can bear it no longer; nothing still but about my faults, my faults! an agreeable subject truly !
>
> *Lord Loverule.* But Madam, if you won't hear of your faults, how is it likely you would ever mend 'em ?
>
> *Lady A.* Why, I don't intend to mend 'em. I can't mend 'em, I have told you so a hundred times ; you know I have tried to do it, over and over, and it hurts me so, I can't bear it. Why, don't you know, my Lord, that whenever (just to please

you only) I have gone about to wean myself from a fault (one of my faults I mean, that I love dearly) han't it put me so out of humour, you could scarce endure the house with me?

Lord L. Look you, my dear, it is very true that in weaning one's self from——

Lady A. Weaning? why ay, don't you see, that ev'n in weaning poor children from the nurse, it's almost the death of 'em? and don't you see your true religious people, when they go about to wean themselves, and have solemn days of fasting and praying, on purpose to help them, does it not so disorder them, there's no coming near 'em; are they not as cross as the devil? and then they don't do the business neither; for next day their faults are just where they were the day before.

Lord L. But Madam, can you think it a reasonable thing, to be abroad till two a clock in the morning, when you know I go to bed at eleven?

Lady A. And can you think it is a wise thing (to talk your own way now) to go to bed at eleven, when you know I'm likely to disturb you by coming there at three?

Lady Arabella goes on to point out with much spirit that hers is by far the more civilized way of life, and when Lord Loverule suggests that 'to go to bed early and rise so, was ever esteemed a right practice for all people', she retorts disgustedly that beasts do it. The quarrel becomes increasingly acerb, until:

Lady A. I won't come home till four to-morrow morning.
Lord L. I'll order the doors to be locked at twelve.
Lady A. Then I won't come home till to-morrow night.
Lord L. Then you shall never come home again, Madam.

We can see there is no subtlety or originality in all this, but there is a certain zest, and the fun is heightened when Lady Arabella recounts her version of the quarrel to her friend Clarinda.

Clar. Good-morrow, Madam; how do you do to-day? you seem to be in a little fluster.

Lady A. My Lord has been in one, and as I am the most complaisant poor creature in the world, I put myself into one too, purely to be suitable company to him.

Clar. You are prodigious good; but surely it must be mighty agreeable when a man and his wife can give themselves the same turn of conversation.

Lady A. O, the prettiest thing in the world.

Clar. But yet, tho' I believe there's no life so happy as a married one, in the main; yet I fancy, where two people are so very much together, they must often be in want of something to talk upon.

Lady A. Clarinda, you are the most mistaken in the world; married people have things to talk of, child, that never enter into the imagination of others. Why now, here's my Lord and I, we han't been married above two short years you know, and we have already eight or ten things constantly in bank, that whenever we want company, we can talk of any one of them for two hours together, and the subject never the flatter. It will be as fresh next day, if we have occasion for it, as it was the first day it entertained us.

Clar. Why, that must be wonderful pretty.

Lady A. O, there's no life like it. This very day now, for example, my lord and I, after a pretty cheerful *tête-à-tête* dinner, sat down by the fireside, in an idle, indolent, pick-tooth way for a while, as if we had not thought of one another's being in the room. At last, stretching himself, and yawning twice, my dear, says he, you came home very late last night. 'Twas but two in the morning, says I. I was in bed (*yawning*) by eleven, says he. So you are every night, says I. Well, says he, I am amazed how you can sit up so late. How can you be amazed, says I, at a thing that happens so often? Upon which we entered into conversation. And tho' this is a point has entertained us above fifty times already, we always find so many new pretty things to say upon't, that I believe in my soul it will last as long as we live.

Here, as everywhere, his women are admirably cool, and get the better of the altercations. Their reasonable unreasonableness is well pictured, and there is great gusto in their portrayal.

For when all is said, if Vanbrugh cannot interest us much in his characters or in his view, his sense of fun, and his broad humour, which he had in abundance, carry him through. *The Confederacy* is full of good and amusing, if superficial characterization, and we get a slightly whimsical sense of the bustling atmosphere of London life. Moreover, we are all agog in all his plays to see how the situation will turn, and it was by cunning devices Vanbrugh held his audiences. He is in his way good fun, but it is rather like that of a pillow fight on a greasy pole above a pool of water. After his domestic scenes, for which he had a real turn, he is at his best in his pseudo-Elizabethan portrayals; in Sir Tunbelly Clumsey who appears armed and attended at his gates; or in Sir John Brute in his cups, disguised as a parson or a woman according to the pre- or post-Collier version. But his comedies are not all of a piece. They are always robust, in burlesque, common morality, or common sense, but he lacked that 'little twist of brain' which makes the comic writer or the satirist, or the literary artist in any sense. He took the writings of others and made what he could of them; he took life as he found it, and left it there.

FARQUHAR.

Born, 1678.
Love and a Bottle, 1698.
The Constant Couple, 1699.
Sir Harry Wildair (sequel), 1701.
The Twin Rivals, 1702.
The Recruiting Officer, 1706.
The Beaux' Stratagem, 1707.
One adaptation from Fletcher.
Died, 1707.

So long as men write in a certain form (inside sufficiently large limits) and with a similar artistic purpose, it is possible to measure them against one another, or to compare

them with some fixed standard. Thus Vanbrugh may justi-
fiably be measured against Congreve. But when comedy
comes to be written with a totally different intent, from, as
far as can be judged, a quite different impulse, the comparison is invidious. We do not try to compare a hollyhock
with a tulip, and it is just as absurd to compare the work of
George Farquhar with the bulk of Restoration comedy. It
is true that in his earlier plays Farquhar accepted Restoration themes and the Restoration manner, but in his last
two, and even in *The Twin Rivals*, he broke away from them.
Certainly to the end he worked the same line as Vanbrugh,
but it is that line most removed from Etherege or Congreve,
namely that of the domestic drama. For the rest, he went
back to Shakespearian times. We may say that at the beginning of the eighteenth century comedy split into two
courses, on the one hand to the sentimental comedy of
Cibber and Steele; on the other, back to the Elizabethans
with Vanbrugh and Farquhar.

Farquhar, it is true, commented upon manners, but such
criticism was only a side issue with him. He was more intent upon lively action and the telling of a roguish tale. It
is all fun and frolic with him, a question of disguises and
counterfeits, the gaining of fortunes, and even of burglarious
entries. 'He lies even further from literature than Vanbrugh', says Mr. Gosse, 'but he has a greater knowledge
of life.' And if his intellect was rather humdrum, he had
flashes of insight. Leigh Hunt said of him that 'he felt the
little world too much, and the universal too little . . . his
genius was entirely social'. But this criticism will only hold
if he is regarded as Congreve's successor, rather than as an
original who projected his disappointments in life—or 'ex-
pectorated his grief', to use a phrase from his single ode—
onto the stage in the form of light-hearted comedy. In his

dramatic world very little is impossible; it is full of Rabelaisian gaiety touched with a satire that is as light as a feather.

A reference has been made to his disappointments, which were these: he failed to realize a competence, and was never accepted among the gentlemen and wits. All his plays contain at least one person who needed at all costs to marry money, and his heroes were more fortunate than he was. The bride who was to have brought him seven hundred pounds a year, proved to be penniless.

Like a true writer of critical comedy he pricked the bubble of pretensions, and did so by thrusting at the wits who would not make him one of them. There are continual strokes at the pretenders to and usurpers of the title of gentleman, or at the false standards by which others recognize them.

When Clincher in *The Constant Couple* is charged with murder and robbery, the constable cries out, 'Murder and robbery! then he must be a gentleman'. But the best touch of all is, 'The gentleman, indeed, behaved himself like a gentleman; for he drew his sword and swore, and afterwards laid it down and said nothing'. There are many hits in the same vein.

The most surprising thing about him is his extreme modernity: many passages might have been written yesterday. He was two hundred years ahead of his time, in the Butler–Shaw tradition when he wrote, 'The patient's faith goes farther toward the miracle than your prescription'; or ''Tis still my maxim, that there is no scandal like rags, nor any crime so shameful as poverty'. On one of the very few occasions when he is at all heavy, he urges that to pay one's tradesmen's bills is more honourable than to pay one's 'debts of honour' incurred at the gaming table. But honour is a prerogative of the wealthy; 'Lack-a-day, sir, it shows as ridiculous and haughty for us to imitate our betters in their honour as in their finery ; leave honour to the nobility that can support it'. But what must appeal to us with peculiar force at the present day are the arguments circling around the question of how much licence soldiers may be allowed at home in return for risking their lives abroad in defence of their countrymen :

> *Colonel Standard.* Had not these brave fellows' swords defended you, your house had been a bonfire ere this about your ears. Did we not venture our lives, sir ?
> *Alderman Smuggler.* Did we not pay you for your lives, sir ? Venture your lives ! I'm sure we ventured our money.

Are not we too, bitterly familiar with the subject of 'war sacrifices'? Or again, there is the scene between Justice Scale and Justice Balance, of which the context is self-evident :

> *Scale.* I say, 'tis not to be borne, Mr. Balance.
> *Bal.* Look 'ee, Mr. Scale, for my own part, I shall be very tender in what regards the officers of the army, they expose their lives to so many dangers for us abroad, that we may give them some grain of allowance at home.
> *Scale.* Allowance ! This poor girl's father is my tenant ; and if I mistake her not, her mother nursed a child for you. Shall they debauch our daughters to our faces ?
> *Bal.* Consider, Mr. Scale, that were it not for the bravery of these officers, we should have French dragoons among us, and that would leave us neither liberty, property, wife or daughters.

How often in recent times did a similar controversy ring in our ears !

The divergence from his predecessors that has received most attention from commentators, is in the matter of love. Mr. Palmer decides that he finally ruined the Restoration tradition by carrying still further than Vanbrugh the 'luscious' treatment of sex. Mr. William Archer, relating the change to modern sentiment in the matter rather than to the earlier, finds Farquhar's cleaner and more rational. His point was that the marriage of bodies, whose joys he would be the last to consider non-important, did involve also a marriage of minds. 'You and your wife, Mr. Guts', Sir Charles Freeman says to Boniface, 'may be one flesh, because ye are nothing else; but rational creatures have minds that must be united', and the end of the play, *The Beaux' Stratagem*, turns upon the separation of the Sullens for incompatibility of temper. Farquhar may have been a gay rogue, but he had common sense, and a tie involving a cat and dog existence such as that led by the Sullens—his rather less literary version of Sir John and Lady Brute—had nothing sacred for him. Separation was certainly better than the brazen cuckoldry practised by the gallants, and used as material by the comic writers of the previous century. The reason, of course, is that social conditions had changed; the assumption that passion and social exigencies could be squared had broken down.

In truth, Farquhar was an advanced rationalist, and this trait comes out again and again in little, subtle touches. He was not to be paid in abstract ideas, or with conventional lies. He realized, for instance, that 'with the estate to back the suit, you'll find the law too strong for justice'. And in this last play there is a touch as good as it can be. Archer has captured the thief Gibbet, and threatens to shoot him rather than send him for hanging:

> *Archer.* Come rogue, if you have a short prayer, say it.
> *Gibbet.* Sir, I have no prayer at all; the government has provided a chaplain to say prayers for us on these occasions.

One would not be surprised to find the remark in a page of Voltaire, and indeed Farquhar was always something of a pre-Voltairean Voltairean, for when at Trinity Dublin he was told to comment upon the episode of Christ walking upon the water, he did so by an allusion to those born to be hanged.

His real divergence, however, consists, as has been hinted, in a return to the Elizabethans. After *The Twin Rivals*, at the period when he saw, and said, that comedy had become but 'an agreeable vehicle for counsel and reproof', he sought for something different. There are passages where one might be reading, if not Shakespeare—although his recruiting court is not far removed from that of Falstaff, and 'profound master Shallow'—at least Massinger or Marlowe in his burlesque moments. He scarcely touches on the humours of Jonson, his Boniface and his Mrs. Mandrake have too much diversity of character. This is not, of course, to belittle Jonson, his is a different and more universal method. Yet listening to Sergeant Kite we might well be hearing some actor of a hundred years before:

> Yes, sir, I understand my business, I will say it—You must know, sir, I was born a gipsy, and bred among that crew till I was ten year old. There I learned canting and lying. I was bought from my mother, Cleopatra, by a certain nobleman for three pistoles; who, liking my beauty, made me his page; there I learned impudence and pimping. I was turned off for wearing my lord's linen, and drinking my lady's ratafia, and then turned bailiff's follower: there I learned bullying and swearing. I at last got into the army, and there I learned whoring and drinking: so that if your worship pleases to cast up the whole sum, viz. canting, lying, impudence, pimping, bullying, swearing, whoring, drinking, and a halberd, you will find the sum total will amount to a recruiting serjeant.

He has an atmosphere of exaggeration that is indeed akin to that of Jonson, but it is of another kind. He is influenced, but he is not imitative. We sometimes feel Bobadill, or

Parolles, or Wilson's astrologer, but he is always original
except in his failures to adapt Restoration treatment. We
may take the passage where an old woman has come to
Lady Bountiful for medicine for her husband, but is inter-
cepted by Mrs. Sullen, who impersonates her mother-in-law.
It begins in the Restoration manner, but flies off to the
heights of a robust tomfoolery :

> *Woman.* I come, an't please your ladyship—you're my Lady
> Bountiful, an't ye ?
> *Mrs. S.* Well, good woman, go on.
> *Woman.* I come seventeen long mail to have a cure for my
> husband's sore leg.
> *Mrs. S.* Your husband ! what, woman, cure your husband !
> *Woman.* Ay, poor man, for his sore leg won't let him stir
> from home.
> *Mrs. S.* There, I confess, you have given me a reason.
> Well, good woman, I'll tell you what you must do. You must
> lay your husband's leg upon a table, and with a chopping knife
> you must lay it open as broad as you can ; then you must take
> out the bone, and beat the flesh soundly with a rolling pin ;
> then take salt, pepper, cloves, mace, and ginger, some sweet
> herbs, and season it very well ; then roll it up like brawn, and
> put it into the oven for two hours.

This is the real spirit of Farquhar, a huge gust of laughter.
Life was a discoloured and painful thing to him, and the
only remedy was to treat it as a game, not the delicate
intellectual game of Etherege, but a good Elizabethan
romp. He is like his own Mrs. Sullen, who ' can be merry
with the misfortunes of other people because her own make
her sad ', but he can laugh at himself as well. Even on his
death-bed, where he wrote his last play, this fierce determination to defeat life, to rise superior to its restrictions and
find an unconditioned freedom, manifested itself in bursts
of boisterous laughter. Pope said that he wrote farce, and
if we accept Dryden's definition that ' Farce entertains us

with what is monstrous and chimerical', this is to some extent true. But he had a most amazing dexterity of touch. He is continually surprising us into laughter with a sudden turn of expression, as when Lurewell in Sir Henry Wildair says:

> Look ye, girl, we women of quality have each of us some darling fright—I, now, hate a mouse; my Lady Lovecards abhors a cat; Mrs. Fiddlefan can't bear a squirrel; the Countess of Piquet abominates a frog; and my Lady Swimair hates a man.

What irresistible ' go ' !

This real Farquhar does not laugh the satiric laugh of the social creature, but the laugh of the child at the unaccountability of things, a laugh that had he lived might have developed into something very deep. His freedom is visible not only in his plots and scenes, but also in his verbal play. This shows itself, not as antithetical wit, but in puns. Here, for instance, we have the meeting between two recruiting officers :

> *Brazen* Have you any pretensions, sir ?
> *Plume.* Pretensions!
> *Brazen.* That is, sir, have you ever served abroad ?
> *Plume.* I have served at home, sir, for ages served this cruel fair—and that will serve the turn, sir.

Or we have a passage where Silvia, disguised as a man, exhibits both the Elizabethan exuberance and the verbal play :

> *Balance.* Pray, sir, what commission may you bear ?
> *Silvia.* I'm called captain, sir, by all the coffeemen, drawers, whores, and groom porters in London; for I wear a red coat, a sword, a hat *bien troussé*, a martial twist in my cravat, a cane upon my button, piquet in my head, and dice in my pocket.
> *Scale.* Your name, pray, sir ?
> *Silvia.* Captain Pinch : I cock my hat with a pinch, I take snuff with a pinch, pay my whores with a pinch. In short, I can do anything at a pinch, but fight and fill my belly.

' He makes us laugh from pleasure oftener than from malice,' Hazlitt wrote. ' There is a constant ebullition of gay, laughing invention, cordial good-humour, and fine animal spirits in his writings.' It is for that we should go to Farquhar. If we search for a poet, for a profound critic of life, for a close thinker of the Restoration type, or for a finished artist, we shall not find him. To approach him for a torrent of semi-nonsensical amusement, mingled with that clear logic which also is the Irishman's heritage, and to ask no more, is to obtain a refreshing release from the conditioned social universe in which we are forced to live.

There remain a few writers of comedy worth more than a passing glance; Wilson, Sedley, Mrs. Pix, D'Urfey, Crowne, and above all Otway, have a certain lasting claim, at least equal to that of Brome in the earlier period, as have the women, Mrs. Manly, Mrs. Centlivre, and, last but not least, the lively and courageous Mrs. Aphra Behn, the worthy companion of the wits. All have a striking family resemblance to one another; they vary in wit, in literary excellence or carelessness, in strength of construction, but they all treat of the same themes—the Frenchified fops, the astrologers, the adventurers, and always with the question, How are we to treat love? But after Farquhar we come to the sentimentalists, who wrote those ' do-me-good, lack-a-daisical, whining, make-believe comedies . . . where the author tries in vain to be merry and wise in the same breath', typified by the works of Cibber and Steele, the latter ' all the time on his good behaviour, as though writing a comedy was no very creditable employment, and as if the ultimate object of his ambition was a dedication to the Queen '. We need not be concerned with Steele, nor with Addison and *The Drummer* here; they belong definitely to an eighteenth- and not a seventeenth-century *milieu*, in which true comedy melted away into the sweetness of tears, or shattered itself upon the pointless crudities of Fielding : for if *Tom Thumb the Great* is a noble burlesque, a play such as *Rape upon Rape* marks a decline as sure and irremediable as *The Tender Husband* of Richard Steele. Collier and the censorship had between them effectively dòne their work.

X

CONCLUSION

IF we were to try to sum up what the comedy of this period as a whole achieved, it would be to say that it gave a brilliant picture of its time rather than a new insight into man. Taine has wondered why, with all its mastery of vivid description, racy idiom, and polished phrase, this English comedy did not come to a fuller perfection, did not reach the level of Molière, and, we would add, of Jonson. Apart from the fact that astonishing genius of every kind is not to be met with in every decade, the explanation perhaps lies in this: these writers never came to the condition of seeing life whole, though what they saw they perceived very clearly. They loved it with Etherege, or, like Wycherley, snatched from it a fearful joy, or, like Congreve, tried in their dissatisfaction to distil from it something exquisite: they hardly ever related it, as Molière nearly always did, to a larger world; they did not try to construct something terrific out of it as Jonson was able to do.

Their time forced them to be too critical, though it is hardly fair to blame a time for the very peculiarities that gave them their best material. But they were forced to be too moral, that is, too engaged with the immediate application of their ideas. It is in this sense that the word moral has been used throughout: nothing so foolish is suggested as that art and morality are incompatible, any more than that they are necessary to one another. Without a moral vision there would have been no *Divine Comedy*, no *War and Peace*. Without the notions of good and evil and divine justice there would have been no Greek tragedy and no *Paradise Lost*. But the morality of the Restoration dramatists, taken as a whole, was not a universal vision; it could not be. For the medieval view was dead, had died in the iron verse of Milton; eighteenth-century scepticism was being born, had made its appearance in the shattering syllogisms of Hobbes and the trenchant strokes of Shaftesbury. Modern curiosity was awakening, and the old moral order lay in ruins about the scaffold of a king. The dramatists of that day were almost necessarily forced to be content with morality as conceived by the *honnête homme*. Wycherley could never imagine, as did Goethe's *Faust*, that all experience whatsoever might be good: Congreve would never see that the art of graceful living might, by its very fineness, miss something fundamental in life, and destroy the directness he was eager to preserve.

These are limitations; but the want of an inspiring, comprehensive philosophy such as was Dante's to use, the absence of a feeling of revolt such as urged Shelley to his most sustained flights, has its advantages. For then the creative impulse is bent inwards upon the thing, it will not be satisfied until the object made has complete validity within itself: it cannot afford to slip into life. Thus lapses into realism which scarcely injure the structure of much Elizabethan comedy are ruinous here, and it is because this kind of perfection requires a more consummate and conscious artistry that so few comedies of this period are satisfactory. Even when complete in themselves they do not always include enough 'spiritual nourishment', to use Synge's analytic phrase, and Etherege's perfect creation, *The Man of Mode*, compared with great comedy, is Sèvres-china painting to a canvas of El Greco. Dryden, more comprehensive, was, except in one great tragedy, always a little too swayed by his experimental curiosity to attain that unity which alone can make such work close-sealed.

But *The Country Wife* and *The Way of the World* are beyond Taine's criticism, and the former can take its place among the great masterpieces of the ages, to stand beside *Volpone*. *The Way of the World* will always remain a trifle isolated, not because it came to so little, but because, working within such severe limits Congreve succeeded in concentrating in it matter for which others have found larger, easier mediums more convenient. It is unique—even if the comedies of Corneille may claim affinity—and likely to remain so, yet it belongs inalienably to its period: it is built upon its contemporaries, and it is by it and *The Country Wife* that the achievement of the period may be measured. It is hard to imagine that in any civilized age they will not be regarded as glories of our literature, gems of our theatrical inheritance.

A SHORT LIST OF PLAYS

AND

A BRIEF BIBLIOGRAPHY

LIST OF PLAYS

THE following list should give a complete enough view of the subject. All the comedies of Etherege, Wycherley, and Congreve are given. The dates are those of the first performance, the editions named the most easily accessible. When more than one is mentioned, the best is marked with an asterisk. For many of the dates I am indebted to Mr. Allardyce Nicoll's full Handlist of Plays at the end of his book (see bibliography).

PRE-RESTORATION.

D'Avenant, Sir William. *The Wits.* 1635.
    (*Dramatists of the Restoration.* Ed. J. Maidment & W. H.
      Logan, 1872–9. 14 vols. D'Avenant, vol. ii.)
Cokain, Sir Aston. *The Obstinate Lady.* 1657.
    Dramatists of the Restoration. Ed. cit.)

RESTORATION.

D'Avenant, Sir William. *The Playhouse to be Let.* 1662.
    (*Dramatists of the Restoration.* D'Avenant, vol. iv.)
Wilson, John. *The Cheats.* 1662.
    (*Dramatists of the Restoration.* Ed. cit.)
Tuke, Sir Samuel. *The Adventures of Five Hours.* 1663.
    (*Dodsley's Old Plays.* Hazlitt.)
Killigrew, Thomas. *The Parson's Wedding.* 1664.
    (*Dodsley's Old Plays.*)
Etherege, Sir George. *The Comical Revenge ; or Love in a Tub.*
               1664.
               She Would if She Could. 1668.
               The Man of Mode ; or Sir Fopling Flutter.
               1676.
    (Ed. by A. W. Verity. Nimmo, 1888. vol. i.)

List of Plays

Sedley, Sir Charles. *The Mulberry Garden.* 1668.

                                 Bellamira, or The Mistress (from the Eunuchus of Terence). 1687.

   (*Works.* London, 1778. 2 vols.)

Dryden, John. *The Rival Ladies.* 1664.

                        Sir Martin Mar-All ; or The Feign'd Innocence. 1667.

                        Marriage à-la-Mode. 1672.

                        The Kind Keeper ; or Mr. Limberham. 1678.

                        Amphitryon ; or the Two Sosias. 1690.

   (Scott's 1808 Edition.)

Shadwell, Thomas. *The Sullen Lovers.* 1668.

                        A True Widow. 1679.

                        The Squire of Alsatia. 1688.

                        Bury Fair. 1689.

   (Mermaid Edition.)

Buckingham, Duke of. *The Rehearsal.* 1671.

   (Edition by M. Summers. Shakespeare Head, Stratford, 1914.)

   Arber Reprints. Constable 1919.

Wycherley, William. *Love in a Wood ; or St. James's Park.* 1671.

                        The Gentleman Dancing-Master. 1672.

                        The Country Wife. 1675.

                        The Plain Dealer. 1676.

   (Mermaid Edition.

   Ed. by Montague Summers. Nonesuch Press, 1924.)

Behn, Mrs. Aphra. *The Town Fop ; or Sir Timothy Tawdry.* 1676.

   (Ed. Montague Summers. Heineman & Butler, 1915. 6 vols.)

Crowne, John. *Sir Courtly Nice ; or It Cannot be.* 1685.

   (*Dramatists of the Restoration.* Crowne, vol. iii.)

D'Urfey, Thomas. *A Fond Husband ; or The Plotting Sisters.* 1677.

                        The Marriage Hater Match'd. 1692.

   (His plays are only to be found separately in old editions.)

Otway, Thomas. *The Soldier's Fortune.* 1680.

   (Mermaid Edition.)

Congreve, William. *The Old Bachelor.* 1693.

                        The Double Dealer. 1693.

                        Love for Love. 1695.

                        The Way of the World. 1700.

   (Mermaid Edition.

   Ed. by G. S. Street. *The Comedies of William Congreve.* Methuen, 1895. 2 vols.

   *Ed. by Montague Summers. Nonesuch Press, 1923. 4 vols,)

Cibber, Colley.   *Love's Last Shift ; or The Fool in Fashion.*   1696.
                     The Careless Husband.   1704.
    (Edition: London, 1777.   5 vols.)
Vanbrugh, Sir John.   *The Relapse.*   1696.
                     The Provok'd Wife.   1697.
                     The Confederacy.   1705.
                     A Journey to London.   1726.   (Posthumous.)
    (Mermaid Edition.
   *Edition by W. C. Ward.   Lawrence and Bullen, 1893.   2 vols.)
Farquhar, John.   *The Constant Couple ; or A Trip to the Jubilee.*
                1699.
                The Twin Rivals.   1702.
                The Recruiting Officer.   1706.
                The Beaux' Stratagem.   1707.
    (Mermaid Edition.)
Steele, Sir Richard.   *The Tender Husband ; or The Accomplished*
                      Fools.   1705.
    (Mermaid Edition.)
Addison, Joseph.   *The Drummer ; or The Haunted House.*   1715.
    (Bohn's British Classics.   Addison's *Works*, 1856.   6 vols.)

BIBLIOGRAPHY

The following short bibliography should give the student a grounding in the subject : [1]

GENERAL HISTORY OF THE PERIOD.

*Aubrey.   *Brief Lives.*   (Clark.   Oxford University Press, 1898.   2 vols.)

*Burnet, Bishop,   *History of His Own Time.*
  Gooch, G. P.   *Political Thought from Bacon to Halifax.*   (Home University Library.   1 vol.)

*Hamilton.   *Memoirs of Grammont.*
Macaulay.   *History of England.*   (Collected Works, Longmans, Green & Co., 1898.   12 vols.)

*Pepys.   *Diary.*
*Spence.   *Anecdotes* (Singer's Edition is the best known).

[1] Of famous books often reprinted, and of books not recently reprinted and difficult to obtain, I have thought it useless to give editions. Contemporary or nearly contemporary works are marked with an asterisk.

Bibliography 177

STAGE HISTORY.

*Cibber, Colley. *Apology,* 1740.

*'Cibber, Theophilus.' *Lives of the Poets,* 1753.

*Downes. *Roscius Anglicanus,* 1708.

 Genest. *Some Account of the English Stage, 1660–1830.* (10 vols. Bath. 1832.)

*Langbaine. *English Dramatic Poets,* 1691. (Gildon's Continuation, 1699.)

 Nicoll, Allardyce. *History of Restoration Drama, 1660–1700.* (Cambridge University Press, 1923.)

 Oldys. (Articles in) *Biographia Britannica,* 1747–60.

CRITICAL.

Cambridge History of English Literature. Vol. viii.

Charlanne. *L'Influence française en Angleterre au XVIIIème siècle.* (Paris, 1906.)

Garnett, Richard. *The Age of Dryden.* (George Bell, 1895.)

Gosse, Edmund. Preface to *Selections from Restoration Dramatists.* (Everyman, 1912.)

Hazlitt. *English Comic Writers.*

Hume, Martin. *Spanish Influence on English Literature.* (Nash, 1905.)

Hunt, Leigh. Preface to Edition of *Restoration Dramatists* (1840).

Lamb. *On the Artificial Comedy of the Last Century.*

Macaulay. *The Comic Dramatists of the Restoration.*

Palmer, John. *The Comedy of Manners.* (G. Bell, 1913.)

Thackeray. *English Humourists of the Eighteenth Century.*

Taine. *History of English Literature.*

Ward, A. W. *English Dramatic Literature* (to the Death of Queen Anne). (Macmillan, revised edition 1899. 3 vols.)

Contemporary Critical Opinions may be found in Dryden's Prefaces and Dedications, especially in the *Essay of Dramatick Poesy,* 1668. (See W. P. Ker, *Essays of John Dryden.* 1900. Clarendon Press. 2 vols.)

Collier, Jeremy. *A Short View of the Immorality and Profaneness of the Stage,* 1698.

Critical Essays of the Seventeenth Century. J. E. Spingarn. 1908–1909. Clarendon Press. 3 vols.

Dennis, John. *Letters on Several Occasions*, 1696.
Farquhar. *Discourse upon Comedy*, 1702.
Vanbrugh. Preface to *The Relapse*, 1696, and *A Short Vindication of the Relapse*, 1698. (W. C. Ward's Edition.)

BIOGRAPHICAL: or Specialized Criticism, besides the Works already quoted.

The Dictionary of National Biography.

Behn.   Summers, Montague. Preface to Complete Edition.
Congreve.   Johnson, *Lives of the Poets*.
               Gosse, E. *Congreve.* 'Great Writers', 1888.
               Ewald, A. C. Preface to Mermaid Edition.
               Street, G. S. Preface to Edition.
               Summers, Montague. Preface to Edition.
Dryden.   Johnson, *Lives of the Poets*.
               Scott, *Life* in Works of Dryden, 1808 (edited by Saintsbury, 1882).
               Saintsbury, G. *Life* in English Men of Letters.
               Saintsbury, G. Preface to Mermaid Edition.
               Verrall, A. W. *Lectures on Dryden.* (Cambridge University Press, 1914.)
Etherege.   Verity, Preface to 1888 Edition.
               Gosse, E. Essay in *Seventeenth-century Studies*, 1883.
               Etherege Letter Book. Brit. Mus. MS. Add. 11,513.
Farquhar.   Archer, W. Preface to Mermaid Edition.
Shadwell.   Saintsbury, G. Preface to Mermaid Edition.
D'Urfey.   R. S. Forsythe. *A Study of the Plays, &c.* Western Reserve University Bulletin. 1916.
Vanbrugh.   Swaen, A. E. H. Preface to Mermaid Edition.
               Ward, W. C. Preface to Edition. [This is the only adequate biography that exists.]
Wycherley.   Ward, W. C. Preface to Mermaid Edition.
               Perromat, Dr. C. *Wycherley, sa vie, son œuvre.* (Félix Alcan, 1921.)

INDEX